WOLVES
AMONG US

WOLVES AMONG US

*Biblical Principles To Identify And
Expose Spiritual Predators*

Linda Reyburn Shirey

Library of Congress Control Number:

ISBN 979-8-89316-871-6 (Paperback)
ISBN 979-8-89316-872-3 (Hardback)
ISBN 979-8-89316-870-9 (Ebook)

1st edition, 2024

Printed in the United States of America

To Dad,

(the) Hal Reyburn,

who made even his enemies to be at peace with him.

CONTENTS

SECTION 2: IDENTIFYING A WOLF

Conflict
Resolution

PROCESS

IDENTIFY

Write a list of specific issues experienced around a certain person or group.

CONFIRM

By prayer, by counsel, and by reading (the Holy Scriptures), confirm that the issue lies outside of personality conflict.

ADDRESS

Using the steps outslined in Matthew 18, address the individual with a specic problem. Be prepared to offer evidence of a real Biblical fault, and offer a path toward resolution.

CLARIFY

If the individual does not hear or understand, bring elders to the next meeting.

CUT TIES

If the issue is not resolved and the unBiblical behavior persists, resolve to either walk away or escalate to authorities.

Additional content: www.coramconversations.com

INTRODUCTION

"Beware of false prophets, who come to you in sheep's clothing, but inwardly are ravenous wolves.... You will recognize them by their fruits."

—Matthew 17:15–20

While I cannot claim originality for this premise, this book is written from the perspective that the most dangerous predators within a church are those who claim to be Christian sheep (i.e., followers of Jesus). Self-deceived wolves work hard to maintain an illusion of sanity, guarding a sense of self and place. If that illusion is shattered, they are left without any identity to claim. The wolves may or may not know that they are sold out to the purpose of evil, but the end result is the same: their involvement in the flock brings destruction. An angry, wounded predator will lash out mercilessly and without restraint.

And they often take the faithful down with them. Faithful, law-abiding people are often the most confused by wolves because the character of the wolf is so completely alien that it feels like dealing with a demented person.[1] In a way, that is an accurate

---

[1] Harry Potter fans may appreciate "Dementor" as a pertinent illustration.

assessment. People can be driven mad by their desires—driven by the overwhelming desire for power. Not every wolf begins by looking like a wolf. It's the subtle ones that get you, and subtlety is Satan's specialty.

Jesus, our Shepherd, commands us to be aware and on guard.

This issue is hardly unusual in the lives of believers, though this particular "fiery trial" can be devastating; it is a betrayal of trust and intimacy.

Even though many others are more academically qualified and formally trained in this topic, I am writing from a personal and observational stance rather than an official leadership stance. I have experienced the turmoil and brokenness of a church split and at least two attempted takeovers, as well as a personal relationship with a predator. I am the daughter of an elder who fought a cult, the wife of a former deacon, and an involved church member.

Mostly I write this as a normal, long-term believer, grappling with life issues that are universally distressing. Many can relate or commiserate; still others have stories far worse. (I hope to hear from some of you because survivors should support each other.)

The observations in this book are the result of many years of prayer, contemplation, observation, Bible study, and countless conversations in the wake of distress-centered living among the tents of the world—and the emotional aftermath of betrayal. Finding actual direction with this other than what my husband calls the "I Love Jesus" sticker approach—"just forgive and all will be well"—tends to be more difficult.

It's especially difficult for solidly Biblical, faithful churchgoers to grapple with the questions of

- Who are the Wolves?

- What does God say about them versus what they say about themselves?

- Why do they come?
- Where do they attack?
- How do you deal with them?

The aftermath of "what do I do now" has shipwrecked the faith of many. They often act like sheep without a shepherd because a false shepherd or a false friend betrayed them. It's distressing but understandable.

Also, a note on victimology: If victim status is being used as a power tactic, there is no reason to feel pity. Not everyone describing a personally bad experience is a genuine sheep being mauled by a wolf, any more than everyone describing an experience with the Holy Spirit is a true believer (see the Biblical example of Balaam the false prophet).

To identify and neutralize wolves, it's critically important to employ the spiritual gift of discernment. If you don't have discernment, ask someone who does. Ask a few someones, such as other law-abiding sheep—and shepherds! Do not be afraid to ask for help in prayer, then explore the normal, ordinary means offered by our Comforter. Doing everything on your own makes you a target, so the group huddle is one of the best defenses used by sheep.

This book is not designed to justify gossip, doubt-creation, or rumor-mongering. Those are the worst tools that Satan ever used to bring down our first family (Adam and Eve), driving a wedge between them and God. And Satan has worked on every relationship with the same tools ever since.

This book is my attempt to put into words the damaging work set loose by our greatest enemy: a wolf with a friend's face. He seduces with words, but he only ever wants dominance through destruction. Men can regress to being something of a beast in human clothing—from Nebuchadnezzar's example to the wild unrestrained behavior of the idol-worshippers at Ephesus (Acts 19; 1 Corinthians 15:32). The Apostle Paul, who fought them, knew their character.

It is my hope to encourage faithful people beset by wolves to ignore the outward appearance in favor of accurate identification, i.e., judging with righteous judgment.

In our weakness, may we be strong (in the Shepherd and Overseer of our souls).

"My soul is in the midst of lions;
I lie down amid fiery beasts—
The children of man, whose teeth are spears and arrows,
Whose tongues are sharp swords.
Be exalted, O God, above the heavens!
Let your glory be over all the earth!"

—Psalm 57:4–5

SECTION 1:
WARNINGS AND CONTRASTS

BEWARE—A COMMAND
TO US FROM JESUS

"Beware of false prophets, who come to you in sheep's clothing but inwardly are ravenous wolves. You will recognize them by their fruits. Are grapes gathered from thornbushes, or figs from thistles? So, every healthy tree bears good fruit, but the diseased tree bears bad fruit. A healthy tree cannot bear bad fruit, nor can a diseased tree bear good fruit. Every tree that does not bear good fruit is cut down and thrown into the fire. Thus you will recognize them by their fruits."

—Matthew 7:15–20

In Matthew 7, our key passage, Jesus explicitly describes the **who**, **what**, **when**, **where**, and **how** of ravenous wolves. But—isn't it curious that The Good Shepherd warns his flock to "beware of wolves"? Why doesn't He just . . . get rid of them?

To return to the passage, it's important to note a few aspects of this central theme:

- Jesus describes an age-old problem beyond sheep versus goats.

- Jesus offers a garden illustration: fruit identifies the heart.

- Jesus indicates the eternal end result of bad plants: fire.

- Jesus repeats the fruit inspection principle for clarity.

- Jesus leaves no ambiguity: "you will recognize them."

This passage describes wolves differently than they would describe themselves (more about that later):

- WHO are Wolves? False prophets.

- WHAT are Wolves? Ravenous.

- WHEN are Wolves identified? By their fruits.

- WHERE are Wolves found? Around sheep (they come to you).

- HOW do Wolves appear? In sheep's clothes.

The only question not answered in this passage is why.

Why are they allowed? This is the million-dollar question that makes everyone nervous. From other passages, this is my best estimate: so God can show His character by contrast, and His glory in overcoming them. Our first parents listened to the original predator in the Garden (a snake), so He's going to teach us knowledge of predators by experience. To prey, there is not much difference between a snake and a wolf.

As with any good manual, let's start with a few warning labels about what will and won't be helpful on the journey of identification and discernment. The warnings cover some basic cultural assumptions and natural areas of hesitation, both of which need to be overcome for sheep to effectively survive their hunters.

Warning #1: Worldly Wisdom Is No Help against Wolves

"The mouth of the wicked conceals violence."
—*Proverbs 10:11*

To deal with evil effectively, one popular modern lie really needs to be removed: "People are all basically good." While God does restrain people in their evil, the shocking thing about wolves is not that they exist. The shock is that the filters of ordinary or "common" grace have been lifted temporarily.

Another modern lie can be used as a weapon for wolves to hold over any sheep's head: "You can't judge the state of a person's heart." By contrast, Jesus's actual words show that identification of inner rottenness is possible. *"You brood of vipers! How can you speak good, when you are evil? For out of the abundance of the heart the mouth speaks"* (Matthew 12:34, Luke 6:45).

Knowing by fruits negates the current Western cultural idea that man's words are of primary importance in determining meaning. While it's wise to assume that humans are not intentionally lying until they are proven guilty, trying to make a Biblical case for man as a blank slate is a hard row to hoe. On a daily basis, Biblical and experiential evidence indicates that man is naturally corrupted.

While most Americans believe that human actions are separate from their natures and are due to forces outside of themselves, Jesus is clearly saying the opposite: healthy and diseased trees produce according to their true nature. He has not said anything about the necessity of digging into an individual's personal historical background or the deep well of his psyche in order to understand him. The Creator understands His fallible creatures quite well. The Lord says clearly that His own nature does not include lying (Numbers 23:19), whereas humans have quite an issue with it (Psalm 116:11).

If the words drip honey but the fruit of the life shows thorns and thistles, that points to a deep and abiding problem of the heart. Thistles and thorns catch on clothing; their purpose is to cling to something tightly, at the expense of the material, in order to ensure survival. If socks are stuffed inside and out with thistles, this discomfort leads to the seeds being picked off or brushed off into any available ground. Sometimes the clothing is so shredded and twisted that it must be thrown away.

Over time, the full trend of personal action and interaction will show the person's heart and state of mind. Wolves will identify themselves.

Warning #2: You Cannot Change Hearts

"The good person out of the good treasure of his heart produces good, and the evil person out of his evil treasure produces evil, for out of the abundance of the heart his mouth speaks."

—Luke 6:45

Despite our technical advances, humans cannot definitively change the nature of a plant. Even with grafting, the wild stock of an orange tree will impart some of that fast, reckless energy to the next generation. Better fruit may emerge after many seasons and much pruning—but one person's influence is not enough to change anyone's heart. That's the work of the Holy Spirit.

Humans are far too weak and sin-laden to accomplish the cure of anything dead or rotten from the inside. It is a particularly odd kind of arrogance that leads people to think that as the reflection of God, they can accomplish all things. The best rebuttal comes from Jesus. *"With man, this is impossible, but with God all things are possible"* (Matthew 19:26).

Wolves may also ensnare you by implying or asserting that you can save them, or the situation. (Example: "You can be the one person who changes everything.") Again, if the fruit of the lips shows a consistent pattern of unbiblical character, Jesus has already said that words overflow from the heart. The spirit of Saviorhood only works with one Person, and He is Divine.

Warning #3: Wolf Profiles within the Pack

"Her princes in her midst are like wolves tearing the prey, shedding blood, destroying lives to get dishonest gain."
—*Ezekiel 22:27*

Not all wolves act in the same way, any more than all criminals break the same types of laws. To identify them correctly, pay attention to what kind of wolf you're dealing with. All wolves seek power and they often hunt in packs, but the way they go about obtaining power might look very different.

The wolf pack itself is like a bitter alliance, always locked in an internal struggle for dominance. The wolves are fiercely fenced against outsiders and loyal to each other, but individuals within the pack can display different characteristics:

- Alpha Wolf—always gathering others to support the cause, leaving destruction in his wake

- Charismatic Wolf—like a snake, operating with force of persuasion and personality with a cold heart (Absalom in II Samuel 15)

- Communicator Wolf – uses words as tools to ensnare, deceive, and destroy (Demetrius the silversmith in Acts 19)

- Wolf-in-Training—a second-in-command forming a pack (Grima Wormtongue)

- Influencer Wolf—like a spider, striking at strategic moments (Denethor from *Lord of the Rings*, or Jonadab in II Samuel 13)

- Loner Wolf—like a victim, appears at odds with himself and in need of help (Gollum)

Essentially, wolves will twist the Scripture to apply in any way that builds their own kingdom. False prophets often make all the right kinds of sheep noises and sounds: humility, discipline, godliness, etc. But the inner drives have somehow become corrupted so they eventually bear the visible fruit of destruction. A ravenous wolf is never satisfied, never content, and above all—seeks power. (Yes, I am borrowing from J.R.R. Tolkien!)

Warning #4: Don't Ignore Red Flags

> *"And they all plotted together to come and fight against Jerusalem and to cause confusion in it."*
>
> —*Nehemiah 4:8)*

Even statements that seem very plausible or justifiable can carry small or large red flags. Say a sheep metaphorically hears warning bells, but it's nothing that she can immediately identify as a threat. When that happens, an inexperienced sheep often assumes that she is wrong or prejudiced in the assumption that something is wrong. She may think, "Maybe I just don't like this person's personality," leading her to believe the warning bell was just personal, not from the Spirit.

But even if she does believe the warning bell and the wrong scent has been identified, the human sheep often plays this mental game: "It can't be that bad—nobody could really mean what I think I heard them saying." . . . But then people get hurt around them. So then she thinks (about the wolves), "They say they don't want to hurt anyone, they just want to help, and it was an accident." But then no one really gets better around them. . . .

Usually, the observer (sheep) will experience conflict between the wolf's words and actions and will feel confused. Despite the warnings, sheep often want to believe the wolf isn't a wolf. Since the words don't match the behaviors of a wolf, the sheep's desire to understand and sympathize with the wolf is usually strong.

To help you not fall into the confusion and to clearly identify the wolf, look for these individual and group characteristics. The special section on response to authority is included because wolves continually seek opportunities to replace legitimate authority with their own.

Individual characteristics of a wolf

- Inadequate apologies. The wolf will not offer full apology in humility for the original offense. He may admit to a related issue, a completely separate fault, or general/inconsequential state of sin or error shared by everyone. But it will be a compelled confession.

- Inflated sense of self. A wolf won't admit a real, tangible fault or consistent personal flaw without a justification qualifier that means he was ultimately right.

- Willful blindness. A wolf will consistently and stubbornly adhere to an idea or a person despite the resulting trail of destruction.

- Extreme impatience. A wolf will have a "my way or the highway" attitude, with no ability to endure hardship or suffering with grace.

- Hypocritical hard-heartedness: Snarling over one instance of historical bad treatment, a wolf will demand that others give grace for his indwelling and unresolved sin.

- Cleanliness/success = Godliness. A wolf will display a fanatical adherence to an orderly, successful, or outwardly impressive life to create a beyond-reproach appearance.

- Demands respect. A driving desire, bordering on manic, to be respected or seen as a teacher/ authoritative influence by others will influence his behavior.

- Lack of peace: There's always another horizon or conquest somewhere; peace is not valued or sought, even temporarily.

Group dynamics of wolves

- No real partnership. Except with their mates or cubs, wolves always see clear winners and losers; no challenge can be met with acceptance or real change.

- Dark charisma. This rip tide of personality hides the fact that others are mere pawns, never trusted equals—or peers.

- Relationship drama. With very troubled relationships lacking give-and-take or contented togetherness, wolves seem satisfied in the midst of chaos, bad news, or conflict. Friends get discarded.

- Legalists. Portraying an outward strict adherence to chief virtues—truth, grace, law, order, meaningful interaction, loving behavior—they create their own legal system just so they can punish any infractions.

- Activity without contentment. Wolves live in an atmosphere of beehive-like tension—non-wolves never know when the bomb will hit, the new idea or new revelation. Restlessness may be explained as (a) keeping things fresh and exciting, or (b) avoiding stagnation.

- Conspiracy. Sheep may be told repeatedly that they have missed the plain-language message about some basic truth because of enemies conspiring to discredit (the wolves); encouragement will be given to listen and believe the wolves' twisted, confusing version without any outside verification.

- Sole arbiters of truth/success. The pack alone holds the message of truth, with the pack leader as spokesman (or spokeswoman). If the promoted formula doesn't lead to a blessed life, then the sheep didn't follow it in the right way, with the right spirit, or some other reason that means "lack of success is your fault." This is a strong feature of the health and wealth gospel message, for example.

Response to authority (by individual wolf or the pack)

- Lack of submission. Wolves usually show a long trail of leaving churches without a clear Biblical cause (citing "lack of fulfillment"), a list of others held hostage to their own personal wounds, or strong resistance to hierarchical systems that don't quickly spot their so-called leadership potential.

- Beyond hierarchy. Any challenge to a pack leader's authority will be met quickly with an identifying label—you are the troublemaker who will need to repent. A system of instant reprisal prevents anyone in the group from challenging the alpha's dominance.

- Demands obedience. Overwhelming and repeated emphasis on Scriptural topics related to obedience: male (dominant) headship/leadership, women's head coverings, children in obedience, or obedience to civil authorities.

- Providing replacements/false helpfulness. Wolves will flatter a leader they think is sympathetic to the cause, circumvent legitimate leaders while trying to build support for their replacement leader, and strenuously deny any claims that they are being manipulative.

Style of Conversation

- Endless debate. Wolves love to argue over inconsequential things dressed up as vitally important topics.

- Kill-or-cure arguments. This "go for the jugular" or "take no prisoners" approach steamrolls all attempts at friendly dialogue because common ground is unnecessary. This goes beyond just a direct approach in favor of a clear attack.

- Failure of real joy. Any emphasis on joyful celebration, beauty, or music will be used as a tool to manufacture or manipulate a specific response.

- Gossip before and after. Knowing the power of words, wolves will go from house to house, spreading unnerving tales of someone's personal failures or a church controversy. "*A dishonest man spreads strife, and a whisperer separates close friends*" (Proverbs 16:28). Even if wolves are disciplined in love, sympathetic listeners will be told that authorities were (a) mean or (b) insensitive or (c) uncaring.

Overall, just know that you will never be able to win any discussion with a wolf, whether it's a principle or a perspective. In their arrogance, the wolf is always, always, always right.

Warning #5: Understand the Exploitation of Weakness

"Benjamin is a ravenous wolf, in the morning devouring the prey and at evening dividing the spoil."

—*Genesis 49:27*

The state of the congregation offers clues about the timing of the attack(s). Wolves often creep in when the flock is scattered, discouraged, lacking leaders, and stressed out. Predators do not fight fairly, and their timing is designed to take advantage of weakness. Thus, it's imperative to stay alert, especially when you're thinking, "Things just can't get worse."

Since wolves will reflexively accuse the other person of wrongdoing, sometimes matching one of the sheep's old weak points or personal wounds (i.e., beating a sheep with a past-history stick), look for a congregation full of historical wrongdoings being mentioned. This is often an area where Satan has already made progress. The wolf will use this knowledge to get sheep into a corner, isolated from friends or family, and go to work on them. The lack of grace will be apparent.

American culture asserts extreme individualism as a strength, but in a contest between sheep and wolves, the "lone ranger" type of individualism is more of a weakness than a strength. Sadly, sometimes sheep will take a brave stand against wolves, and get tossed around in the ring as collateral damage. Wolves are spiritual predators in physical spaces. If the sheep assert their self-deterministic rights in the might of their own understanding, and not in the armor of God, they will fall down like ninepins.

Sometimes, the Good Shepherd binds their wounds, repairs their broken legs, and sends them back into battle once they agree to wear God's armor. Sometimes, He calls them home. He does not always shield His sheep from the consequences of willfully and repeatedly walking down the road to destruction.

To add a note of comfort and encouragement, one of a predator's major fears is to be wounded (made vulnerable), weakened, or left unprotected from other predators. They fear receiving the same treatment that they've dished out.

Predators fear becoming the prey they devour. When predators seem invulnerable, remember that they have fears—so, therefore, they also have weak points that can be exploited.

> **Predators fear becoming the prey they devour**

Warning #6: Don't Waste Your Love and Patience

"Purge the evil person from among you."

—I Corinthians 5:13

Inside a church community, God calls us to correctly identify and drive out rotten elements from our congregations.

However, when this concept of "purging the evil person" is applied, it's often done badly. Man's strength, cleverness, or kindly patience is not enough to drive out wolves, nor can sheep overwhelm wolves with niceness. (Overcoming evil with good does not mean allowing sin to continue without consequences.) It does not help that sometimes the wolves hide behind the letter of the law.

Misusing Christ's command to forgive as a cloak, wolves often deceive churches into administering cheap grace instead of discipline. That false idea—the offering of cheap grace—has robbed much of the church of her Christ-ordained strength and influence. It has also allowed wolves to escape with zero consequences for their deep and abiding sin of rebellion and desire for preeminence.

Dietrich Bonhoeffer defines cheap grace in this way:

> Cheap grace means grace as a doctrine, a principle, a system. It means forgiveness of sins proclaimed as a general truth, the love of God taught as the Christian "conception" of God. An intellectual assent to that idea is held to be of itself sufficient to secure remission of sins. The church which holds the correct doctrine of grace has, it is supposed, ipso facto a part in that grace. In such a church the world finds a cheap covering for its sins; no contrition is required, still less any real desire to be delivered from sin. Cheap grace therefore amounts to

a denial of the living Word of God, in fact, a denial of the Incarnation of the Word of God.

Cheap grace means the justification of sin without the justification of the sinner.[2]

The entire book of I Corinthians is instructive, but chapter 5 verse 13, in particular, warns against allowing sin to bear bad fruit unidentified and uncorrected. In context, Paul is saying that those bearing fruit unworthy of the kingdom are supposed to be disciplined. This concept has been lost over the years, but failing to remove bad fruit is actually unloving to the rest of the flock; by neglect, the flock is encouraged to wander around without protection. It is unkind for leaders to let egos balloon beyond restraint.

> *"But now I am writing to you not to associate with anyone who bears the name of brother if he is guilty of sexual immorality or greed, or is an idolater, reviler, drunkard, or swindler—not even to eat with such a one. For what have I to do with judging outsiders? Is it not those inside the church whom you are to judge? God judges those outside. 'Purge the evil person from among you.'"*
>
> —*I Corinthians 5:11–13*

Later, Paul underlines this idea by saying that the *unrighteous will not inherit the kingdom of God*, and warns people about being deceived.

---

[2]   Dietrich Bonhoeffer, *The Cost of Discipleship* (New York: Collier Books, 1963), 45–46.

Warning #7: Judge by Their Fruit

"Do not judge by appearances, but judge with right judgment."
—John 7:24

With all these warnings, you might think it impossible to really identify a wolf. What if you make a mistake? Only with the help and discernment of the Holy Spirit can true identification occur. Even though the primary means of identifying a wolf is not by outward appearance, wolves often use two outward-focused tactics to ensnare sheep: paranoia and legalism.

Paranoia is based on the fear of man (what will others say or think?) and legalism is based on works righteousness (I am good because I have done good actions). Legalism is what happens when people are more concerned with maintaining outward appearances than being holy and set apart for God's purposes.

A few Biblical examples tell us that it is possible to pierce the fleecy disguise of wolves without falling into the deadly trap of either paranoia or legalism.

- The prophet Samuel pierced through Agag's false desire for peace, quite literally (I Samuel 15:33).

- The civil leader Nehemiah pierced through the disguise of Shemaiah the son of Delaiah, who tried to sell out his leader to the enemies of God (Nehemiah 6:10).

- Christ Jesus has contended with our greatest enemy, Satan, and visibly shown His superiority over His enemies by defeating Death (let alone Judas) (Romans 6:9, Revelation 1:18).

Real love includes addressing an issue of truthfulness with clear, unobstructed sight, as far as it lies within us. We are to be *"wise as serpents and innocent as doves"* (Matthew 10:16) in confronting and addressing the issue. And of course, the famous "judge not, lest ye be judged" passage is essential because it requires self-judgment before addressing another's issue.

Where Is Our Hope?

> *"Therefore take up the whole armor of God, that you may be able to withstand in the evil day, and having done all, to stand firm."*
>
> —*Ephesians 6:13*

Our enemy is not silent—nor should he be ignored—but our Lord is also ever watchful and alert because of those who truly fear Him.

Revelation says . . . Jesus wins. Jesus has already won on the cross. We just have to endure the fiery trial and keep alert. And don't turn your back on the danger and run; it's the worst thing you can do.

IT'S INEVITABLE: WOLVES IN THE CHRISTIAN COMMUNITY

"Brothers, the Scripture had to be fulfilled, which the Holy Spirit spoke beforehand by the mouth of David concerning Judas, who became a guide to those who arrested Jesus . . . For it is written in the Book of Psalms, 'May his camp become desolate, and let there be no one to dwell in it,' and 'Let another take his office.'"

—Acts 1:16–20

While maintaining or encouraging predators is unbiblical, it's also not the job of the church to prevent every bad person or circumstance. The Lord said we would experience real horrors on Earth: bad doctrine, false teachers, physical and spiritual hardship, etc. Though Christians are not fatalists, shrugging shoulders and hopelessly intoning, "Whatever will be will be," we can trust that He does have a real purpose for this trial.

While being wise as serpents and harmless as doves, we also have a duty of self-protection. We are not to walk up to the wolves and offer ourselves as living sacrifices (i.e., don't go too far in the passive acceptance of a wrong). Remember that since God is Judge, He will ultimately right that wrong, though He has appointed judges and counselors and other authorities to dispense a measure of His eternal decrees. If they fail or if they attempt to destroy the flock, they will be held to account.

It's also okay to be persistent in asking for justice, as the widow did with the unjust judge in Jesus's parable (Luke 18:1–8). We are allowed to accurately complain if our guards are abusing their authority. Their appointment as guards does not make them ultimate judges.

In His infinite wisdom, God allows His church to look weak and unimpressive to the world and to Satan. Sometimes, wolves are lured into a decrepit-looking enclosure just to get thoroughly beaten up by the Shepherd. While it's inevitable that wolves will come, both II Peter and Jude show that the end of all false teachers is destruction in the day of judgment.

Why Are Wolves Allowed to Invade Flocks?

The question of "why" is perhaps the most difficult (and the most important) for us as believers, but the first step in understanding the *why* requires faith in a just, righteous, and loving God. Since Jesus invited a predator to become one of the original 12 disciples, my premise is that, in addition to fulfilling prophecy, He wanted the other 11 disciples to develop an ability to identify a wolf within a wooly disguise. Showing can be more effective than telling because even when the disciples were told things, they did not always immediately understand.

Long after Christ told his disciples about wolves in church life, they finally recognized their personal betrayer: Judas. Judas wasn't the only disciple to betray Jesus: Peter denied his association three times on the night of Christ's arrest. However, the main difference between Judas and Peter is that Peter repented. He lived a life of sacrifice and suffering, exactly as his Lord had modeled.

Through the template provided by Judas, we see the difficulty in identifying a wolf and why a predator cannot be allowed to remain near the sheep. The disciples also lived out the heart-searching that happens when sheep wonder if they are the problem (*"Is it I, Lord?"*). Betrayal is a very awful form of persecution; it's mentioned nine times in Matthew 26 alone.

Yet, despite Judas's betrayal, Peter and the rest of the disciples remained true and Jesus's ministry flourished. It is inevitable that we will have wolves in our congregation, but just like the disciples, we can prevent the wolf from creating too much damage as long as we use the power of contrast, imitation, and discernment.

- Contrast—we can see the difference between our old master (Satan) and our King and Lord (Christ).

- Imitation—we can better model Christ as we work to drive out the sin that would turn us into wolves.

- Discernment—we can identify the unrestrained desires in wolves and avoid their dreadfully familiar patterns (i.e., their activities sometimes look like standard inclinations but without barriers, stretched to the furthest extent that they can go).

Developing a healthy disgust and rejection of wolves, from their root to their fruit, is part of our sanctification. Sin, which would destroy us and everyone around us, is not always easily identifiable. Like the difference between a psychopath and a normal human being, a wolf in a congregation is simply someone who shows little to no restraint or hesitation in following the most self-serving human impulses. They have a terrible self-centered logic to everything they do. It's twisted, it's malformed, and it's evil.

The first step toward purging evil in the group is to identify it as evil.

Why Are Wolves Allowed to Destroy?

> *"Not only that, but we rejoice in our sufferings, knowing*
> *that suffering produces endurance, and endurance produces*
> *character, and character produces hope, and hope does not*
> *put us to shame, because God's love has been poured into our*
> *hearts through the Holy Spirit who has been given to us."*

> —Romans 5:3–5

We might be able to find Biblical justification or reasons why God allows wolves to invade the flock, but it's harder to understand why He allows them to destroy. Does He ever directly describe His purpose in the allowance of suffering? The books of Judges and Acts contain many (painful) examples, but it may be easier to see contributing factors than causation.

As indicated in the book of Job, it's difficult to prevent questions from taking a turn for the worse. Questions may begin with God's methods or use of normal means, and turn into an attack on His character. It may be a natural but unwise question to ask, "What kind of God allows His own beloved bride to be torn?"

In Judges, the wolves have so deceived the Israelite sheep that they are hopelessly addicted to idols and imitations of the surrounding nations. Israel is nothing like the people God has called them to be, and the church has been severely damaged. The cycle of sin becomes really clear—God's people sin, wicked adversaries are allowed to cause trouble, God sends judges, sin is confronted and beaten back—then God's people sin again. Rinse and repeat. Thus, as a corrective measure, God may allow wolves to cause trouble to bring a congregation's focus back on Christ. It is harder to get distracted from your Protector when someone wants you dead, and it's harder for predators to pretend friendship while also destroying.

As a means of building faith through suffering, Acts contrasts the heroic feats of the apostles empowered by the Holy Spirit with the indwelling stubbornness of God's chosen people. One of the most dynamic examples is of Paul's life after his conversion on the road to Damascus. In Acts, Luke repeatedly describes Paul's custom of visiting synagogues and telling his fellow Jews about the claims of Jesus. What do they do? Try to kill the messenger. Hey, it worked in Jerusalem, so let's try again. (To be clear, this is not a response relegated to one group—the Gentile worshippers of Artemis/Diana tried this exact approach in Ephesus, as described in Acts 19.)

Throughout its history (e.g. Judges and Acts), the church has clearly suffered damage. This can lead us to question God. But if we acknowledge that God is righteous and loving, we know that His actions and purpose will shape those goals of righteousness and love. In this life of sanctification, God is working to:

- Reveal stubbornness: Sin is a hardwired, embedded addiction. If we are not constantly aware of its siren call, it will turn our spiritual walk into nothing but talk. God reveals not only our stubborn sinfulness but also uses His church to reveal the wolves He warns us about.

- Test faith: God tests the hearts and minds of His people, both to show His goodness and to show us how much we need Him. This testing proves the faith of His people, while also showing the unfaithfulness of wolves.

- Establish restoration: Everything earthly will pass away—but He is reserving for us a glorious and incorruptible hope of inheritance. Regardless of what God's church suffers on Earth from wolves, we know that He will restore all things. The wolves that crucified Christ could not keep Him in the grave.

Suffering tests faith so that the good fruit of hope can fully flourish—when it is linked to the undying faith that God intends trials for our good. Hope is the evidence of things invisible. Hope comes from the unlikely combination of God's wrath, the fruit of rebellion (both of men and of angels), God's mercy and love, and His justice.

Sometimes people act like this is an easy process—of course, Christians want character and hope. Of course, God means everything for our good. Just do the right things, and good things will come to you. If you're doing the wrong things, you'll be punished, Romans 13 says so. Easy!

Maybe . . . not so easy. When the difficulty of struggle through sufferings is acknowledged, it can be encouraging to read somewhat-ignored passages in the Old Testament that follow the sequence of sin, suffering, restoration, and the Lord's vengeance on enemies. Lamentations 3 is one passage illustrating the difficult path of hoping in the Lord alone. Verses 4 and 14 sound like Job's sufferings, from the skin wasting away to becoming a taunting song of worthless men. Verse 48 (*"my eyes flow with rivers of tears because of the destruction of the daughter of my people"*) sounds very much like Jeremiah 8:21. Verse 53 (*"they flung me alive into the pit"*) sounds like Joseph crying in a pit for the crime of being his father's favorite—because his brothers hated him for the real vision of leadership that was given to him by God. It sounds like David's deep cry to be released from God's wrath and all "workers of evil" in Psalm 6.

This third chapter of Lamentations indicates that it is good, but not easy, to wait quietly for His salvation. He will wound, and He will bind those wounds. Because of the issue of sin, we—like justly-convicted prisoners—don't have the right to complain that God is unjustly allowing bad treatment on Earth. Our first parents (Adam and Eve) sinned—betrayed—rejected—and listened to one other than God. Every one of their children carries on that legacy to some degree.

We wait in these twilight times, between already (Christ has finished His work on the cross) and not yet (our final inheritance has not yet appeared). It's not an easy place to be. It feels like walking a tightrope, and sometimes it feels like God is expecting us to perform for Him.

The reality is that He has already created the kingdom, but for His people to rule and reign with Him, they must develop the character and skillset of good rulers. As co-heirs with Christ, we inherit the kingdom that He built; through suffering, He burns away the dross that keeps us from having the character of good rulers.

As our Savior and example, Jesus will enact final judgment on our enemies. *"You will repay them, O Lord, according to the work of their hands"* (Lamentations 3:64). This means that wolves' destructive ability has an end point. The suffering is temporary; the hope is eternal.

God Is in Charge

The tightrope of temporary suffering above the solid ground of hope is illustrated by the person of Job, in the book of Job. Even when using every available tool to destroy Job, Satan wasn't able to accomplish his goal, for the very good reason that God really had established a hedge of protection. Even while every other comfort, encouragement, and earthly incentive was removed, Job's faith remained. God restored all that He had taken away—as was His right to do.

The drama of Job 2 is that everything is supernaturally destroyed or removed from one person on the same day but through ordinary means. Fire. Raiding parties. Tornadoes. There is nothing unusual about Satan using multiple tools bound in a "miniature sick society"[3] to accomplish his goal.

Job definitely has points of repetition. By the end, one inescapable point is that the Lord alone retains the right to authority. He has the right to tell humans why they are obligated to Him for life. He has the right to tell Satan what he is and is not allowed to do. Absolutely no one is allowed to call Him to account. He is a self-managing, self-directing, entirely sufficient spiritual Being who has created everything that we can and can't see. He is the original definition of Good who has provided the person and example of His opposite (evil) for instruction. He is the original, and Satan mimics everything that He does—for envy and spite.

Satan and Co. always attempt to sound as if they are beings of light who deserve good treatment. Jesus saw Satan fall from heaven, and that showoff has always tried to pretend that he can come back in if he wants.

---

[3] M. Scott Peck *People of the Lie* (New York: Touchstone, 1983), 124.

WOLVES VERSUS SHEPHERDS: BIBLICAL EXAMPLES

The Pentateuch makes it tough to maintain a perspective of perpetual progress. God's people experience a lot of downs on the way to the ups.

Wolves on Fire: Israel's Rebels versus Moses

> *"Is it a small thing that you have brought us up out of a land flowing with milk and honey, to kill us in the wilderness, that you must also make yourself a prince over us?"*
>
> —*Numbers 16:13*

Sometimes cockiness is its own worst enemy, and sows seeds of its own destruction. When a leader receives criticism, consider the source before blithely proclaiming, 'where there is smoke, there must be fire'. A leader does not always deserve the critique that he gets, though he is flawed.

In Numbers 16, leaders Korah, Dathan, and Abiram (and On, son of Peleth) represent two tribes plus 250 *"men of renown."* They ask what seems to be a logical, democratic question of the basis for Moses and Aaron's leadership status: *"For all in the congregation are holy, every one of them, and the Lord is among them. Why then do you exalt yourselves above the assembly of the Lord?"* (Numbers 16:3).

The following exchanges show that these accusations actually fit the behavior of these "men of renown" in trying to replace God's appointed leaders. Echoing the anthropomorphic figures of wisdom versus foolishness in Proverbs 9 that offer the same advice (*"Whoever is simple, let him turn in here"*), both sides throw similar warnings at each other: *"You have gone too far"* (Numbers 16:3,7).

On the third round of dispute with Aaron and Moses, Dathan and Abiram explain what's really on their hearts. They point the finger of blame away from themselves and toward Moses: *"You have not brought us into a land flowing with milk and honey, nor given us inheritance of fields and vineyards"* (Numbers 16:14). As with Jesus's disciples who promoted a "seeing is believing" philosophy (John 7:3-5), Dathan and Abiram show that critique is not the same as proof of wrong. Moses wasn't wrong and didn't deserve their critique.

And the Lord is on his side, as he tells Moses and Aaron to clear the area around the tents destined for earth-swallowing, burning doom. *"And fire came out from the Lord and consumed the 250 men offering the incense"* (Numbers 16:35). To the people packed in a ring around the wolves in Numbers 16:24, God offers a second chance at life. But another 14,700 clearly don't accept God's judgment, and complain against Moses and Aaron: *"You have killed the people of the Lord"* (Numbers 16:41). They get one extra day of complaint before dying horribly of plague.

Exodus, Leviticus, and Numbers show that Moses is not the people's problem—he continually stands between them and God's persistent stated desire to destroy them for a host of sins, including grumbling and complaint. His chosen people are not content with anything that God provides in the desert: food, shelter, mates, leaders, or methods of worship.

The upside to this story is that the sons of Korah apparently escaped their father's end. The sons of Korah went on to become famous temple singers and servants of the Lord. Just because you grew up around a wolf, or you supported a wolf at one point in time, doesn't mean you have to continue on that path.

Balaam: False Prophet Extraordinaire

"Forsaking the right way, they have gone astray. They have followed the way of Balaam, the son of Beor, who loved gain from wrongdoing, but was rebuked for his own transgression; a speechless donkey spoke with human voice and restrained the prophet's madness."

—II Peter 2:15–16

The next hurdle for the Israelite pilgrims is a renowned sorcerer and false prophet-for-hire named Balaam, contracted by the king of Moab to curse the people of Israel. In Numbers 22, we see an established wolf at work alongside another wolf. The only shepherd clearly identified in this story is the Lord.

Balaam is visited by honored Moabite princes; their king, Balak, wants Balaam to curse the people of Israel. To put this in a more modern context, this would be like asking a voodoo expert to put a hex on a group of a few million people. Balaam was viewed as someone in touch with powerful spirits able to cause considerable damage.

Since Balak is also powerful, Balaam does not reject the Moabite princes' words outright. Hinting at consideration of their proposal, Balaam shields himself by passing the buck to a higher Power (*"as the Lord speaks to me,"* Numbers 22:8). He holds this plan B in reserve for any hint of trouble: *"The Lord has refused to let me go with you"* (Numbers 22:13). In addition to being a cop-out, it's also a way of muddying the waters regarding the speaker's true intent.

On the second visit from greater dignitaries, Balaam uses the smoke-and-mirrors method. (*"I could not go beyond the command of the Lord my God to do less or more . . . please stay here tonight, that I may know what more the Lord will say to me"* Numbers 22:19.) Since the Lord had already told Balaam not to go with the Moabites or curse His people, he already knew the Lord wasn't going to change his mind, but this is his way of shifting blame. Balaam's words seem transparent, but they are hiding an intent to repackage God's Word to work Balaam's will. It's blame-shifting at its finest. "It's the Lord's fault I can't give you what you want" versus the direct alternative that Balaam never used: "I won't curse the Lord's people no matter what you offer."

Numbers 22 really identifies Balaam's defects as a prophet. He ignores God's instructions to wait until he is called to go with the princes of Moab. He is blind to the angel with the flaming sword. He fails to understand the donkey's uncharacteristic resistance, and he expresses a wish to kill the messenger. When he beats his speaking donkey and then tells her, *"You have made a fool of me,"* Balaam's character is established as a single-minded, dedicated member of the "take care of number one" club.

The wolf's actual words mean nothing. Balaam's will to finish the project speaks louder than any cautionary words expressed to the Moabite leaders. The angel has to flat-out tell him that his donkey saved his miserable hide by having the sense to fear an angel with a flaming sword. Per M. Scott Peck's observation in *People of the Lie*, evil is "surprisingly obedient to authority."[4]

Balaam continues his selective sight and hearing by offering this powerful authority figure the right words: *"I have sinned, for I*

---

[4]   Peck, *People of the Lie*, 180.

did not know that you stood in the road against me. Now therefore, if it is evil in your sight, I will turn back" (Numbers 22:34).

This sounds like the Israelites' reasoning prior to their defeat in Numbers 14: Let's use sin words, look repentant, and maybe we'll get our way.

Yet even when he's following God's instructions, Balaam can't resist manipulation. He goes to high places used for Baal worship, rather like Satan offering his best temptation to Christ on a very high mountain (Matthew 4). Then when Balaam orders the Moabite king Balak to build seven altars, with bulls and rams, it's clear who is giving the orders. Numbers 24:1 makes it clear that Balaam is trying to game the system to the very end: *"When Balaam saw that it pleased the Lord to bless Israel, he did not go, as at other times, to look for omens, but set his face toward the wilderness."*

Don't mistake God's use of Balaam as a mouthpiece under compulsion for a real prophet. *"Let me die the death of the righteous"* did not happen in his own life (Numbers 31).

A wolf giving up a battle he can't win doesn't mean that the sheep win the war. It means that he's retreating to fight at a more opportune time. Since he found that enchantments won't change God's mind, he finishes as best he can. Balaam blesses Israel, Balak screams at him for a job badly done, and Balaam hides behind plan B as if he's obedient to the word of the Lord.

If obedience is not voluntary, it's not real. Forced obedience without the heart is mere compliance.

Hophni and Phineas versus Samuel:
Wolves in the Flock and Their Human Shields

"Then in distress you will look with envious eye on all the prosperity that shall be bestowed on Israel, and there shall not be an old man in your house forever. The only one of you whom I shall not cut off from my altar shall be spared to weep his eyes out to grieve his heart, and all the descendants of your house shall die by the sword of men. And this that shall come upon your two sons, Hophni and Phineas, shall be the sign to you: both of them shall die on the same day."

—*I Samuel 2:32–35*

Failure to apply discipline has a ripple effect and creates a long-term impact on a greater community of believers. There is no victimless crime.

Up front, we're told that these priests of the Lord were *"worthless men"* (I Samuel 2:12). Hophni and Phineas had created a completely self-centered system that involved them sending a proxy (the priest's servant) to forcefully take away parts of sacrificial offerings before they were acceptable in God's sight. Not only did they poison others against engaging in sacrifice, but also they violated the women who gathered for prayer meetings.

Did their father, the chief priest, restrain or remove Hophni and Phineas after the many bad reports? No. Instead of applying discipline to his sons, father Eli soothed his conscience by analyzing this *fama clamosa* (prevalent report of scandalous or immoral conduct by a church member) and wagging an admonishing finger: *"No, my sons; it is no good report that I hear the people of the LORD spreading abroad"* (I Samuel 2:24).

Clearly unimpressed with Eli's methods, God sent two witnesses to call him to account: an unnamed prophet and a reluctant, underage child (Samuel). The Lord was not shy in speaking words of His own: The appointed high priest had honored his sons over the Father, allowed his sons to blaspheme, and scorned His sacrifices. Further, God holds Eli to account with a multi-generational curse, removing the blessing of old age and adding heart-wrenching sorrow and starvation: *"Please put me in one of the priest's places, that I may eat a morsel of bread"* (I Samuel 2:36).

Later on, when the ark had been snatched by the Philistines, Eli was described as "very heavy." The Word drew attention to Eli's weight, not as a health issue but as a heart issue. The unnamed prophet's words about Eli and his family *"fattening yourselves on the choicest part of every offering"* (I Samuel 2:29) are an indication that he personally gained from the wickedly obtained sacrificial offerings. On the same day that Hophni and Phineas were executed via the hands of the Philistines, God exacted justice by causing Eli to fall to his death.

It's easy to call for justice in the generic, and then get shocked when it arrives in a specific instance because the consequences are so severe. Wasn't Eli just being overly kindhearted? Wouldn't it be hard to remove your sons from their positions, disgrace them in front of the community? It's easy to point to particular groups outside of your own and say, "Why didn't **they** deal with this problem early on? How could **they** fail to act?"

It's much harder to say to friends or colleagues, **"You** are no longer able to serve as a minister because you did something (or didn't do something). **You** let your child continue to engage in youth ministry, though there are troubling reports of abuse. **You** did not stop a deacon from using church funds for personal use. **You** failed to blow the whistle on a fellow elder for berating his wife in front of guests. **You** have public temper flares and never apologize. **Your** sermons were plagiarized. **You** will step down or be removed." Yet the difficulties are necessary, and weighing the cost keeps people from making false accusations.

Eli's real problem was that he ignored three levels of warnings sent to him by God. One, he ignored the importance of the people's reports by failing to remove his sons from their positions. Two, he failed to heed the warnings and the curse applied by both prophets sent to him specifically. Third, he turned fatalistic when Samuel brought confirmation that the Lord would wipe out his entire household line as punishment. His sons were so far gone in wickedness that there was no sacrifice left for them, and Eli was so far gone as a leader that God preferred to send His prophecies to a frightened child than the appointed high priest.

Eli's response to Samuel's prophetic message sounds like acceptance of God's will: *"It is the Lord. Let Him do what seems good to Him"* (I Samuel 3:18). However, Eli did nothing to indicate he wanted to make amends with the Lord or even step away from the office himself. Real repentance involves real change, and real change is personal.

Something similar happened with Samuel. From I Samuel 8, it's possible to infer that Samuel picked up bad habits by living around two generations of corrupt priests. Following the pattern of Hophni and Phineas, Samuel's sons, Joel and Abijah, were also worthless men who *"took bribes and perverted justice"* (I Samuel 8:3). Possibly Samuel unwittingly passed on what he learned from Eli, Hophni, and Phineas, or maybe he just wasn't at home long enough to see the character of his sons before appointing them as judges. Either way, his sons' character became the justification for the elders to demand a king (I Samuel 8).

Samuel was a great priest and prophet, but no one's sin operates in a bubble. Both Eli and Samuel lived to see their sons' rejection of the Lord, and neither of them chose to publicly discipline their sons.

Sometimes when wolves repeatedly get away with astounding behavior—skating out of problems that would usually bring severe consequences—someone close to them is engaged in the cover-up. Once the human shield has been dealt with, it's possible to go after the wolves.

Pharisees and Sadducees: Ambitious Wolves versus Jesus

"You see that you are gaining nothing. Look, the world has gone after Him."

—John 12:19

Jesus dealt with the worst wolves of them all, up close and personal: Pharisees and Sadducees. While it's culturally acceptable to hurl behavior-based accusations of "being a Pharisee," the Scripture is clear that both Pharisees and Sadducees wanted to kill Jesus for speaking the truth: He was the Son of God, and they had no part in the kingdom of heaven. They were angry because they were accurately identified as predators by both Jesus and John the Baptist ("ravenous wolves," "brood of vipers," "child[ren] of hell") rather than sheep. They wanted affirmation and validation of righteousness in the worst way possible.

The Pharisees and Sadducees provide an excellent example of wolves in positions of temporal and spiritual power, resembling their true father of lies. They were controlling and ruthless, not caring about either the health of the flock or the intent of the words pronounced by Moses the friend of God. They did not consider their own inconsistencies and resented hearing them described by Jesus. They joined forces with other groups they despised, such as the Herodians (Mark 3:6), in order to take down their real enemy.

> Once the human shield has been dealt with, it's possible to go after the wolves

35

When seen fully in action, they were busy attacking Jesus with questions at every public opportunity, lying in wait to catch him at vulnerable times or in some sort of inconsistency. Blinded by hatred and loss of face, they sometimes attacked each other with cries of "you are gaining nothing." Finally, they moved on to attempted murder, and then actual murder.

The Pharisees and Sadducees began well but ended badly, possibly to show that initial zeal can be turned to real and lasting harm. They brooked no dissent in their war of one-upmanship with the Lamb of God, ignoring any miracle or sign that didn't fit their preconceived notions, and they actively attempted to cut off the voice that opposed them. Crusading against the evils they saw in their law-breaking congregations, they became the evil they first sought to eradicate.

In John 9, the Pharisees display a curious pattern after hearing about God's work in someone's life. Jesus performs a miracle by opening the eyes of a man born blind. When the man is brought to the Pharisees, their first action is to collect his statement about the circumstances of the event. Then they argue over how to label Jesus based on the timing of the miracle. Third, they grill the blind man about his perception of Jesus. Fourth, they badger his parents with assessment questions because they don't believe the healed man's account. When the frightened parents point back to their grown son for answers, the Pharisees recall the healed man for another interview and demand that he label Jesus a sinner, rather than "a prophet."

In the wake of these leaders are consistent signs of conflict, confusion, and doubt.

Their words sound pious (*"Give glory to God,"* John 9:24), but it seems more likely that they are annoyed at not finding any holes in the account of healing. The healed man, possibly annoyed that everyone wants to argue about his personal history, points out the lack of belief: *"I have told you already, and you would not listen. Why do you want to hear it again? Do you also want to become his disciples?"* (John 9:27). In contrast to his parents, he seems well beyond caring about public rejection, possibly because the Pharisees never lifted a finger to heal (or help) him. Unable to answer his questions, the Pharisees cast him out of the synagogue . . . although Jesus later finds him, and worship happens anyway.

So why did Jesus allow for these wolves to become leaders of the flock? One, it provides a publicly visible contrast between the true Shepherd and the worthless shepherds who will eventually be destroyed. Two, the contrast offers an opportunity for change; the Pharisees' determination to find a flaw in Jesus did create an equal and opposite reaction in the healed man. His position shifted from "Jesus is a prophet" to "Jesus is the Son of God" in short order.

When dealing with wolves who have reached a position of power, remember who really makes lame beggars to walk and the blind to see. The sign of Jesus's coming is increased health, healing, and restoration of truth. Clearly, the restoration of truth, and His description as someone *"gentle and lowly in heart"* (Matthew 11:29) does not preclude the application of strong words against abusers of authority.

When the temple is praised for its beauty, Jesus tells his disciples, *"There will not be left here one stone upon another that will not be thrown down"* (Mark 13:2). The Pharisees spent a good bit of time building up their image and allowing money-changing thievery for the sake of the temple.

God removes the valued possessions of those who use His service for their own gain.

Simon Magus: Lone Wolf with Ambition versus Peter

*"Pray for me to the Lord, that nothing of what
you have said may come upon me."*

—Acts 8:24

Some wolves with ambition, like Simon Magus (Acts 8), will join a group just to get something out of it. The type of advantage may differ, but sometimes the attraction lies in gaining social credibility, whether through the development of business contacts or the veneer of respectability and influence. Perhaps wolves want to gain access to children, which is why many church nurseries do background checks on volunteers. They may be attracted to the funds or the people, and use a position of authority to gain access and influence over them. In micro groups, they might love the idea of being a big fish in a very small pond, as a means of leapfrogging into higher positions.

Can we use Simon the Magician as a predator example and call him a fraud—or was he just a flawed follower of Christ? Isn't that an instance of begging the question? He did ask for prayer, after all.

When the gospel came to Samaria, Simon lost his audience. Suddenly, the crowds *"with one accord paid attention to what was being said by Philip, when they heard him and saw the signs that he did* (Acts 8:6)." The crowds had previously paid attention to Simon, and now they were being baptized into a new form of belief. In short order, Simon is baptized, sees miracles, and is amazed. But when he sees Simon Peter and John applying the power of the Holy Spirit on these newly baptized believers in Samaria, the desire to recapture his former status takes over.

There are other red flags indicating that Simon Magus' level of belief was not tied to a real level of repentance:

- Prior to his profession and acceptance into the Christian community, this magician called himself great, while crowds called him *"The power of God that is called Great"* (Acts 8:10). This man was not in need of acceptance.

- By attempting to buy the true power of God, Simon wanted to own and control the Holy Spirit for his own personal advantage; it is hard to imagine a stronger blasphemous insult (Mark 3:28–30).

- While Simon Peter wrestled with issues of pride, he could clearly see the sin of pride and bitterness wrapped around Simon Magus like a choking noose. As appointed leader of the apostles, it was Simon Peter's right to openly challenge Simon Magus's sin.

- This was the second time that Simon Peter had destroyed someone's money-driven ambitions (see Ananias and Sapphira's story in Acts 5).

- While he stated it as a possibility, Peter never guaranteed that Simon Magus's heart issue would be forgiven. The only future projection that Peter made in this whole interaction was *"May your silver perish with you"* (Acts 8:20).

- Apparently afraid that Peter's curse would stick, Simon's response sounds like a veiled demand to avoid consequences and does not include admittance of sin: *"Pray for me"* (Acts 8:24).

It's likely a blessing that we never hear about Simon Magus again.

Simon Peter left us a template for dealing with the wolf's ambition: squarely punch it in the nose. There is no quiet or kindly appeal to reason; no admonitions about a higher and better way of being that will really make a dent. The most you can hope for is to instill a sense of cautious restraint via clear boundary lines that are patrolled frequently.

> Simon Peter left us a template for dealing with the wolf's ambition: squarely punch it in the nose

Give the wolf a reason to be a bit more cautious in pursuing its intended pleasure by offering a painful experience. There's a reason for setting traps along well-used travel routes.

Personal Example

I once interacted with a very charismatic young wolf who put on a very good show of real repentance, expressing a desire to join our congregation to worship Jesus. On his second or third round of regular attendance, he expressed a desire to attend a family camp and interact with other believers. Mum and I took him along, and he regaled us with sordid tales of Uber and Lyft driving; we gave him sensible advice in our turn. After family camp, he expressed an interest in an elder's daughter. Mum and I told him that she was a bit outside his league, so he asked for help—and I gave him a stack of books and movies that might help him strike up meaningful interactions.

Not many weeks later I found out from an international friend (studying for a high-level degree) that she had been approached by this same person. After some baring of the soul to each other, he apparently asked if she had considered a "friends with benefits" situation. I was furious because he had received my help in pursing an elder's daughter, only to turn around and try for an easier mark in the same small congregation. It was cynical, it was abusive, and I had had enough of his hangdog "oh if only I could change" appeal. He did not want to change. He didn't join to seek repentance and worship; he joined to find women to prey on.

The next time I saw him, I glared at him as if my one desire was to punch him straight in the nose. I saw him speaking with yet another woman in the parking lot and warned him off by text, saying that he had no business spending any amount of time with single women because of his well-known personal boundary issues. I warned her that he was not a person to be trusted. Since his conduct was under review by the elders, our very new pastor told me to stop communicating with this person, which I gladly did. Eventually, he was excommunicated. He had repeatedly used one of his friends as a Father Confessor, and had shown a real lack of desire to actually turn from his chronic sin issues.

My conscience has not bothered me about any of these interactions, because this young man was a bona fide menace. If he had shown aggression in any way, I would have felt fully justified in using any legal tool to be rid of him, and I would not have asked for permission before taking action.

Wolves do not learn anything from interactions like these, except to hide their intentions more effectively.

Wolf Pack: False Authorities versus Paul

"You will indeed hear but never understand, and you will indeed see but never perceive . . . Therefore let it be known to you that this salvation of God has been sent to the Gentiles; they will listen."

—Acts 28:26–28

41

Dealing with a pack of wolves can be exhausting. Sometimes, you have to know when to call it quits and refuse to deal with the group, even if some seem willing to listen.

In Acts 28, the Apostle Paul finally decides to leave his fellow Israelites to their own devices. He had reasoned, begged, and pleaded. He had offered all evidence that pointed to Jesus as the Messiah. He had experienced sleepless nights and threats to his person. Yet all the Israelites wanted to do was nitpick and argue and engage in divisive tactics to avoid seeing the truth.

Paul finally issued a prophetic curse. Shaking off the dust of his feet against his own countrymen, he affirmed the prophecies in Isaiah 6, indicating that the despised Gentiles would receive the message largely rejected by Israel—and thus receive their inheritance. It's clear from other New Testament writings that Paul would have removed a limb for his people if they had been willing to listen. This is the power of love and self-sacrifice that wolves consider to be a weakness.

In Galatians, Paul (and others) did not accommodate the false brothers' demands after their habits had been clearly displayed. These "leaders" only wanted to bring the sheep into their own brand of slavery. After the experience with Judas and the Sanhedrin, the apostles were not about to submit themselves or the church to false authority, and neither should we.

When it seems like the wolves are winning, remember: God's weakness is stronger than man's strength (I Corinthians 1:25). Despite the way that wolves make their prey feel—alone, helpless, and weak—we have The Good Shepherd who fights in unconventional ways. Though his work is thorough, this does not mean that every flock will be retained in its original form. As in the diaspora mentioned in John 7 and James 1, sometimes He scatters the flock and then starts again, very patiently, to teach them a real form of dependence on Himself. New Testament believers were sent out to spread the gospel beyond the holy huddle.

The church is only built on the good news and work of Christ, not on the work and wonder of man. That's why He chose those lacking in strength, lacking in wisdom (I Corinthians 1:26), and lacking in philosophy or worldly knowledge (Colossians 2:8).

Over the course of time, God will be proven right. All the tactics and maneuvers, the undercutting and snaps at people's reputations, will prove fruitless as well as completely unworthy of a member of the kingdom.

HOPE: THE GOOD LEADER (AND COMMUNITY) PROFILE

"You then, my child, be strengthened by the grace that is in Christ Jesus, and what you have heard from me in the presence of many witnesses entrust to faithful men, who will be able to teach others also. Share in suffering as a good soldier of Christ Jesus."

—II Timothy 2:1–3

In contrast to a wolf-bitten congregation, a healthy congregation will remember that Christ is the ultimate head of the church. Sometimes when dealing with enemies intent on remaking your community after their own image, recall the original template and the original image.

Underneath Him were appointed the 12 apostles, who in turn delegated some authority to deacons and appointed elders of their own. This provided the framework of the original early church, which was built roughly along the same lines as the Old Testament Aaronic priest-and-Levite system.

The Apostle Paul ordered Titus to appoint elders in every town where he was working as a pastor (Titus 1:5), thus passing on the system and the mantle (so to speak). In two letters to Timothy, Paul outlines the qualifications of church officers (I Timothy 3).

In contrast, Paul describes conflicts with self-deluded leaders such as Hymenaeus and Alexander, *"whom I have handed over to Satan that they may learn not to blaspheme"* (I Timothy 1:20).

Sub-Shepherds

True appointed leaders act as sub-shepherds. They follow the path of the ultimate Shepherd, leading as he would.

They are not called to rend and tear and remake the flock to their own personal satisfaction or rebuild it in their own image of what ought to be. Neither are they to capitulate to every whim of the sheep, who are easily confused and upset.

Care for Sheep

> *"I am the good shepherd. The good shepherd*
> *lays down his life for the sheep."*
>
> —*John 10:11*

Being valued for your usefulness is not the same as being valued for your self. While wolves appreciate the use of human shields, they do not value and support those who need a great deal of care and help. Thus, the mark of a real shepherd is his care for the sheep, whether or not they are of any earthly use to him (or the cause).

Sub-shepherds are to exude love for the sheep, not cold calculation for their own profit, with justifications attached.

Hirelings use the congregation for their personal benefit. Perhaps they focus on building a bunker for their personal use— or gathering tithes that are funneled toward the leader's personal home. No explanation of the "need for ministry" can cover that sort of outright greed.

Self-Sacrificial

> *"Greater love has no one than this, that someone*
> *lay down his life for his friends."*
> —John 15:13

Real shepherds give up their lives for the sheep; it costs them something to serve. These sub-shepherds have been appointed by Christ (originally) to defend the flock with their own lives.

Matching Paul's pattern (*"I am talking like a madman"* in II Corinthians 11:23), they rarely remind others of their great sacrifices. You know them intimately and personally because they give of themselves, not just of their ideas meant for others to implement.

On the other hand, hirelings—those who treat God's calling like a corporate job—expect the sheep to give up their lives for the sake of their leaders or the cause. The sheep end up bearing the brunt of the cost.

Publicly Repentant

> *"But the tax collector, standing far off, would not even lift up his eyes to*
> *heaven, but beat his breast, saying, 'God, be merciful to me, a sinner!'"*
> —Luke 18:13

Sub-shepherds are not afraid to do what they should be telling their flock to do: admit their flaws publicly, personally, and repeatedly. They do not think they are "the next Martin Luther"[5] or something close to Jesus personified. To use a historical

---

[5]   This was a phrase used by a cult leader, in my family's hearing, to describe the importance of his own efforts in the movement he intended to create.

example, William Wilberforce was not afraid to ask that God be merciful to him, a sinner. Sounds like the repentant tax collector, doesn't it?

Hirelings are quick to tell their flock what to do but rarely follow their own advice. They usually ask for mercy when they have been caught in a flagrant violation of God's laws or man's laws.

Confident in Christ

"And David said, 'The Lord who delivered me from the paw of the lion and from the paw of the bear will deliver me from the hand of this Philistine.'"

—I Samuel 17:37

Sub-shepherds may doubt their own talents or abilities—flocks are hard to manage—but they have confidence in God and the power of His might. They are not afraid, after having done everything they can do, to leave results in His hands. Anything else would constitute double-mindedness (James 1:8), in which you continually give the problem to God and then take it back.

Far from doubting or critiquing themselves, hirelings reserve their doubt and critique for others. Skilled at blame-shifting, hirelings are quick to point out others who have violated (or appear to have violated) norms and procedures, while they sit on a hilltop and comment on the actions of the peasants and underlings below. They do not suffer from lack of confidence, but from lack of self-control and character.

In Conflict Designed for Resolution

"When you draw near to a city to fight against it, offer terms of peace to it."

—Deuteronomy 20:10

Sub-shepherds endure, but do not thrive on, conflict. While this is an unavoidable facet of church life—because humans cannot converge without discovering differences from others—conflict should not be an endless cycle. There should be reprieve points and areas of rest. A good shepherd desires peace but has the courage to stand fast in his convictions when attacked. They may struggle with fear of man but refrain from reflexively labeling those with other perspectives as heretics.

Hirelings have a habit of haranguing or vilifying—cursing comes first and blessing is reserved for those who are of personal use. (Some branches of Christianity experience this type of egotism from leaders who believe themselves to be too "anointed" to suffer any critique.) The strong tone masks a great fear of man disguised in bravado.

Sub-shepherds can leave a good legacy without obsessing over it. A manipulative leader will obsess over his reputation or legacy because he wants to manage others' impressions even as he has gone on to his eternal reward. A good leader will act with the understanding that if he acts with consistency of character and principles, God will sort out the legacy.

Personal Example

My father once acted as an occasional substitute preacher in my childhood congregation. His series on the difficulties of double-minded Lot left an impression. Dad talked about how continual hesitation and resistance to God's stated intentions made Lot ineffective in his walk, although he was counted as a righteous man. He tried to reason with angry, lustful crowds. He tried so hard to convince people to leave a doomed town, he endangered himself and his family—dragged out by angels. After he saw the burning rubble of the city where he'd lived, he turned hermit—

and incestuous grandfather. Failure marked his steps, as Lot did not practice consistency in his faithfulness.

When my father was one of two elders holding together a wounded congregation, the wolves came under cover of unity and respite. I have a very clear memory of Dad teaching Sunday school, all calm on the outside, repeatedly clicking a pen in his right hand while the lead wolf and his acolytes schemed and plotted and endlessly interrupted.

The stressful, long battle of occupation ended in the wolves pulling back into themselves, slandering my father's name in our city, and occasionally appearing like specters at funerals or in homeschool groups. Dad never descended into rudeness, but he didn't allow the group to come back. Eventually, he received an apology and admission from one of the invaders that the group coming to "rest and rejoin" was indeed a takeover attempt. Later on, two families who had been involved in this group realized they needed to leave, were shunned, and joined our congregation. It wasn't the end of the story, but it offered a type of resolution.

Faithfulness can help you last out a siege. Consistency can help you rebuild from rubble. Double-mindedness means you leave the rubble behind and barely escape with your life.

Signs of a Healthy Community

The Bereans are often used as an example of a healthy community because they *"received the word with all eagerness, examining the Scriptures daily to see if these things were so"* (Acts 17:11). They provide a contrast to the Thessalonians, who agitated crowds with the goal of ridding the region of Paul and Silas, those Jesus-preaching pests.

The Bereans from the Macedonian region are praised for their *"contribution for the poor among the saints at Jerusalem"* (Romans

49

15:26). In II Corinthians 9 and 11, Paul uses the Macedonians' zeal as a way to encourage the distracted Corinthians to do what they had promised for a year: provide a substantial gift for struggling believers.

With those in the leading Macedonian city of Philippi, Paul goes into detail about *"giving and receiving"* (Philippians 4:15) as a sacrificial act, well-pleasing to the Lord. The generous spirit of Barnabas ("son of encouragement") seems evident, rather than the grasping spirit of Ananias and Sapphira.

In the same way that a bad trip can require more detail than a trip where everything goes as planned, a good flock may be easy to identify (and require less involvement from its leaders) because things happen the way they should.

Indicators of a church operating *"decently and in order"* (I Corinthians 14:40)

- The service runs like clockwork, and the leaders make it look easy. (It's not.)

- The people serve with a genuine spirit of gratitude rather than escaping at the end of the worship service as if their house is on fire.

- Children can sit quietly where they are told, without acting like a twenty-minute sermon is akin to a root canal procedure. (This takes training.)

- There is humor without drama, and helping without harm.

- Prayer meetings (and other means of grace) are attended faithfully and with genuine appreciation, even if the group is small.

Indicators of genuine fellowship

- Congregants act like they want to be where they are (not elsewhere).

- People make plans to meet outside of regular worship or service times, simply because they enjoy each other's company (and not to plot against their current leadership).

- In conversations about subjects of mutual interest, you may hear comments about a recent sermon, topic of Bible study, or chat with non-church members about spiritual matters.

- Congregants are interested in each other's lives outside of the work of the church, and may candidly disagree on secondary topics, such as politics or personal choice.

- Leaders may make intentional steps toward building bridges with other groups or denominations.

Indicators of Christ-centered acceptance

- New members will not feel as though they need to perform to become a "real" member of the church.

- Demographics may include a variety of ethnic backgrounds, training, and social levels, without visible discomfort or clearly delineated lines.

- Conviction levels may differ without bringing salvation or sanctification into question.

- Old members do not feel the need to describe the dirty laundry of the congregation or dwell on all the historical issues leading to the current state of distress.

- Former members are sad when compelled to leave and look forward to visiting when they return to that area (rather than reliving bad memories in the parking lot).

One of my father's favorite books was written by a genuine shepherd turned pastor (*A Shepherd Looks at Psalm 23*). In it, he describes sheep who will not lie down unless all difficulties have been removed from the "green pastures" (pests, sounds, etc.) and who require "still waters" because they become agitated around water bodies with any movement. Shepherds must develop the art of patience because sheep are easily startled, confused, and disoriented—and can harm themselves quite easily. (This would not be news to any church leader.)

In short, it is a minor miracle to find a congregation munching quietly, scattered across a hillside without fear, near streams moving at any speed. While they will sometimes butt each other in play or in earnest, they can mill around in a group without anyone starting a fight. Life and peace are possible if the mind is set on the Spirit rather than the flesh (Romans 8:6).

May the words in Acts 9:31 be your reality:

So the church throughout all Judea and Galilee and Samaria had peace and was being built up. And walking in the fear of the Lord and in the comfort of the Holy Spirit, it multiplied.

SECTION 2:
IDENTIFYING
A WOLF

CHARACTERISTICS: IDENTIFYING A WOLF'S PROFILE

I t's easy to spot criminals *after* they've broken the law, following a trail of well-written reports. It's hard to know in the thick of things, especially if your judgment has been shaky in the past.

It has never been an easy task to spot a wolf inside the fold until the pattern gets overwhelming. They are incredibly convincing in their borrowed fluffy robes. Since they don't carry a visible brand on their foreheads, it will not be easy for those doing the uncovering.

In the *Lord of the Rings*, J.R.R. Tolkien points out that the shadowy enemy of Middle-Earth (Sauron) is just a servant. He has servants of his own (orcs, goblins, lead wizard Saruman, etc.), but in essence, Sauron has a master. In the same way, wolves are merely servants of the real enemy.

If you are feeling foolish for your inability to see more clearly, or for giving grace that was abused, consider the 12 apostles. Judas was not identified as the betrayer until *after* the damage was done.

Our Lord had a good reason for this lead-up to the big reveal. No one really put two and two together regarding the missing funds until after the betrayal. Maybe Judas said things a little too confidently or was a bit careless with money, but don't we all have character flaws? He certainly seemed repentant afterward, returning the blood-soaked 30 pieces of silver, except that his next act was to avoid blame and responsibility. He just bowed out.

A Wolf's Nature

While sheep are not naturally known for their intelligence or foresight, manipulators are hard to spot. Just remember the sequence of fruit inspection: (a) *"Wisdom is justified by all her children"* (Luke 7:35) and (b) *"You will recognize them by their fruits" (Matthew 7:16).*

False words

- Wolves work hard to appear to be what they are not. Their words not only hide any keys in self-identification, but also they mask true intent.

- Wolves know the words to say to gain an audience.

- Wolves identify and isolate the sheep on the fringes of the fold, those who long to engage meaningfully or more deeply.

Con artist to the broken

- Wolves gain the confidence of hurting people who feel embarrassed or guilt-driven.

- Wolves do not maintain genuine interest in people who oppose them, their ideas, or the cause.

- Since the yes-people take years to leave the cage and tell others about the experience, those outside this dangerous inner circle often don't know the extent of the bad situation until years have passed.

Non-material influence

- The "gain" sought by wolves is not always measurable or material (power, control, authority).

- Wolves use esoteric or easily misunderstood doctrines to either undercut an accepted tenet or completely revise it.

- Without much outright opposition, followers will insist the new doctrine is (a) necessary (b) more Biblical (c) more attractive to new converts or (d) logical.[6]

Fear of mistaken identity or false judgment

- Assessors need proof of damage, which means the damage has already happened (bad fruit has already been produced).

- Wolves will use a genuine shepherd's reluctance as opportunity to misidentify him as weak; if a leader delays in applying discipline, out of a desire to allow seeds of repentance to bear fruit, the wolf will exploit this hesitation by increasing harm to the sheep.

- Endless second chances without consequences is a cultural norm, not a Biblical one. The expectation that everyone claiming the name of Jesus will automatically want the right things is a failure to deal with ongoing sin matters.

- Since no one but God can judge the heart with absolute accuracy, wolves will use this truth to

---

[6] If you begin with a bad premise, logic will not help you out of a ditch. It will stand at the edge and tell you in a cold, calculating voice that it is right for you to be in the ditch. If logic is law-focused, the same voice will gladly condemn you for your sin, as an easy target. If logic is grace-flavored, it will keep you in the ditch while singing in beautiful haunting melody about the incredible freedom you're experiencing without healing the brokenness.

bludgeon their opponents who ask to see fruit. "You can't judge me" means "you can't criticize the results of what I'm teaching."

Ignorance

- Most sheep believe they do not have authority to do anything about the wolf because they cannot carry out discipline on their own.

- Lack of knowledge about church history encourages wolves to recirculate discredited doctrine, rebranding damaging heresies as "something new" without opposition.

- Apathy

- Some apparent followers of Christ actually hate Jesus as the ultimate authority; they use His Word to build their own following out of envy or strife. The apathetic sheep will say to themselves, "At least the Word is being preached."

The center of the wolves' existence is pride, otherwise known as arrogance or hubris. They will never truly admit to a wrong. Even when admitting to a fault, they always find someone else to blame—they always have a "but" or an excuse.

- I had the right to do this.

- I was just responding to someone else's sin.

- I got tempted unfairly.

- Anyone else would have done this if they'd been in my particular shoes.

- The other person was worse.

- That was when I wasn't a true believer.

- It was for a good cause.

- It was for the other person's good.

- The bad press isn't real/people are just envious and vindictive about our success.

- It didn't really happen this way (i.e., you don't understand).

- I grew up with a bad background; no one taught me any better.

- The world is bad and getting worse. We have to contend constantly—eggs get broken making omelets.

- My boldness is godlier than your wimpy avoidance of conflict.

If wolves have suffered, the cause can be distilled down to a few reasons:

- Self-induced: They pursued an unrealistic goal and got shot down.

- Mountain out of a molehill: For years, wolves will howl about a small amount of bad treatment as if they were sold into slavery.

- Activism: After becoming involved in a good or trendy cause, the effect of their involvement was unappreciated—most likely because it was an unwelcome power play.

- Cross-fire: They got caught in someone else's problem.

This point cannot be over-emphasized: No one can really believe anything that is spoken or written by the wolf because it does not match reality. Rather like the fig tree that so frustrated Jesus, the fruit of the wolf's doings speak much louder than his words, which are intended to deceive.

While it's noble to think the best about someone until you know otherwise, it's foolish to throw caution to the wind and welcome a wolf with open arms. Conversely, this does not mean you must be filled with suspicion or guarded in every interaction. Just don't ignore the red warning flags waving or the bells clanging in the back of your mind. Deal with them. Talk to someone, preferably a trusted authority figure.

Appearances are Deceiving

If you're hoping for wolves to admit a wrong or volunteer their true purpose, you'll be waiting forever. Most of what wolves do is an act, a calculated performance. If you surprise them into a genuine or revealing move, it will not be pretty. It certainly won't have anything to do with real vulnerability.

As cave-dwellers in deep places, wolves make it very hard to flush them out of their dens. Like foxes, they often have multiple exits. When cornered, they try to distract by feints and rushes, to see if there's an opening for escape. When wounded, they snarl and may coordinate attacks, with one leaping for the jugular while another is slashing at the legs.

For these reasons, it is not possible for a sheep to make enough overtures of goodwill, openness, or transparency for wolves to see the light. They will see kindness as an opportunity to rend, tear, and destroy—as Saul did before he became the Apostle Paul. Jesus withstood Saul on the Damascus Road in the most public way possible: took away his eyesight and forced him to become visibly dependent on everyone but himself.

There is never enough purity in worship, brotherly affection, work of the Spirit, or bond of peace to satisfy wolves. Their destructive existence is threatened by the Shepherd. Overcoming evil with good, in this case, is simply a matter of showing them they are wrong, engaging in verbal battle publicly, excluding them from any position of authority or influence, and protecting the flock against their

> There is never enough purity in worship, brotherly affection, work of the Spirit, or bond of peace to satisfy wolves

attacks. In the kingdom of God, their purpose is to provide a contrast to the real sheep following the Shepherd. The sheep are called to persevere until Judgment Day.

Motivation: Deceit and Disobedience

It takes time to sniff out these predators and find something that just doesn't quite "smell right" about the wolves' attitudes, habits, responses to stress, and responses to under-shepherds. It won't be one thing but many threads woven together.

- The wolf is for the wolf. As a false prophet, his goal is to spread false doctrine, so he is often gifted with words. The longer the wolf sits in a church chair or pew, the more problems that church will have. Why? Because the wolf's primary motive is disruption, and his primary purpose is to thwart authority. The wolf wants to live under no one's authority but his own. This is why some wolves start their own churches, in a house by themselves, without anyone looking over their shoulders—other than those "of the same mind." In that case, no one would be left with whom they disagree, so no one would challenge them and win.

- The wolf pretends to be under submission while kicking against the goads (see Jesus's admonition to Saul in Acts 26:14). This makes wolves hard to sniff out because as a thinking sheep, each believer has a small howler in the back of their own head. It's not hard to relate to this behavior because the problem of substitution (man's will for God's will) has plagued our human race since our great grandcestors were driven out of the Garden of Eden.

  Think about the aftermath of the flood in Noah's day. Noah's family had survived every rejection phase for 100 years of his preaching about the end times. They were preserved as the world drowned and waited with him for signs that watery judgment was abating. Quite literally, this one family of eight souls was the only one supporting Noah as he obeyed God's command to build an ark. Yet, this initial obedience did not stop Noah's own son from turning into a predator after the flood was over. After *"Noah awoke from his wine and knew what his youngest son had done to him"* (Genesis 9:24), a generational curse was applied to Ham, one of the other seven members of the only house church on the planet.

  This is a sobering reminder: The heart of a wolf can emerge from the person who has stood by you in time of need. No one gets an immunity clause.

- The wolf is intent on places of authority. Sometimes wolves sneak into a leadership position by a show of submission, offering their pale underbelly to a leader without showing his teeth—until the leader's back is turned. Once a wolf is established in a hierarchy, they will take care not to be rejected or isolated. While lone wolves can either exist as outcasts or ambition-driven dominators (like Cain in Genesis), sometimes they band together with a "misfits" title to give each other hope and protection against other wild creatures.

- The wolf offers anti-establishment rhetoric while often acting as personally authoritarian. Wolves may appreciate a hierarchical structure or the requirements of a code of law in theory. But in reality, they neither believe that current shepherds are implementing it correctly, nor will they adhere to any real authority structure outside of themselves.

If a wolf is part of a group that encourages structure, he will always maneuver for a position of authority while behaving like a maverick. A wolf becomes visibly pleased when "winning" against someone in genuine authority over them, as if he'd won the lottery or been given an island. It's a little frightening and different from having a competitive streak. It's as though they really believe they cannot lose. They will fight like demons for personal advantage.

This is one reason why churches are often beset with wolves who want to gather a group before they leave, with either other outcasts or deluded sheep. These sheep are not viewed as beloved friends. They are seen as food and protection against the cold, uncaring world.

Personal Example

A pair of wolves once told me, with glee, how they issued an outright threat to a kind and introspective elder in my home church. Essentially, they were glad that they'd bludgeoned him with the stick of conscience: "You're trying to force us to be silent against conscience, so that's proper grounds for us to leave this congregation." According to their rendering, he blanched to the roots of his hair in shock and backed off of his position. They'd won the day, and the conversation shifted toward them getting what they wanted, using the "weaker brother" argument as a weapon.

To my shame, I replied something about the change in position, that obviously they had forced him to see the issue in a new light, but something about that interaction bothered me other than the sense that my response was neither candid nor wholly truthful. At the time, I felt vaguely queasy, like I'd just seen a lion go leaping after prey, and somehow by sitting still beside the camera, I'd contributed to the wounding and tearing. Like picking up a shotgun and offering a warning shot, I ought to have challenged them on the spot: "Obviously you don't care about the effect you had on this person. Why were you so unloving?"

It seemed clear to me that they were so glad to have gained a position of power that the person meant nothing. It was doubly convicting because I've seen myself act that way and then justify it under the rubric of principle over people. Jesus does not do this. He challenges on the basis of principle with the betterment of the person in mind.

Various complex lies were embedded in this interaction:

- Gaslighting: The way they were describing this man's character did not match the person that I had known for many years. They were trying to brand a patient, longsuffering person as a tyrant.

- False superiority: Their excitement in sharing something that should have remained private was an indicator that they felt I was part of their in-group, allowed to share secrets and play along with the takeover games.

- False portrayal of a sensitive conscience: They did not see anything wrong with issuing threats to those in power. This was part of their pattern of dismissing anyone's abilities outshining their own.

- Superiority complex: The female wolf, in particular, took pains to tell me that her spouse was equal or superior to our pastor in intellect and wisdom. Essentially, all she needed to get from the pastor was understanding and empathy, or "pastoral care." I tried to indulge the hope that she would grow out of this tiny tyrant mentality, but that hope proved to be false.

At the very least, if I had spoken up, I would have been excluded from the in-group. At most, I may have drawn fire or painted a target on my own back. In hindsight I think those options would have been worth standing up to them because resistance to a common enemy is encouraging to shepherds. Men in leadership, who have to deal with this sort of power-play nonsense, need all the support that they can get against those who deceive and disobey.

Lack of Love—Words as Weapons

"To them we did not yield in submission even for a moment, so that the truth of the gospel might be preserved for you."
—Galatians 2:5

Wolves deceive the faithful into not trusting each other. When brothers and sisters are more guarded against each other than against their enemy, they can turn Christ's sacrifice into a reason to beat each other with words. I have learned to be wary of those who encourage believers to pit their knowledge against one another. It benefits no one but those who thrive on disagreements over petty things. I once heard a prominent leader say something really profound about the nature of the church split that deeply affected the church of my childhood: "I saw two groups of people who did not love each other."

If one main indicator of the church's faith is the way its sheep and under-shepherds love each other, then a main indicator of rebellion is how much Satan's band hates God's people and each other. They rend and tear and destroy, doing so in the name of Christ and the purity of His church because His name is powerful. They only understand the language of power.

Confusion and Separation

> *"And they were very sorrowful and began to say to Him one after another, 'Is it I, Lord?'"*
>
> *—Matthew 26:22*

Even after the threat has been identified, the wolf really counts on conscientious and tenderhearted people to doubt their own instincts. When Jesus shared with His apostles that one would betray him, they asked each other, *"Is it I, Lord?"* While self-examination is a normal part of the believer's life, causing doubt, fear, and self-examination are a wolf's favorite tactics and not a reflection of our Savior. Gentle people will start to think they've been unkind, strong people think they're being weak, contemplative people think they're stupid or undiscerning, and gracious people think themselves hasty and judgmental.

Sometimes the confusion arises because sheep don't want to understand that the charismatic speaker is really steeped in self-centeredness. The speaker may have gained trust by repeating the right phrases, obtaining a high position of leadership, or gaining a reputation for a holiness on spiritual matters far above the average believer. Some groups describe charismatic leaders as "gifted from on high" or "anointed" to a special position. The leader's every word matters. And because of that, they cause others to examine their faith or search beyond usual limitations. They can even make people feel like they owe their spiritual progress to the leader's training.

To gain trust, wolves will *say* they've suffered for taking a stand against all the things that real sheep are told to avoid. Because of their charismatic nature, it's easier to believe their words. Plus, it's not pleasant to think that these leaders are saying one thing and meaning the complete opposite; but consider the outcome of the words. They may talk about bringing clarity, but all the wolves cause is confusion and division. They may use a lot of words or concepts that don't really match some of the plain truths of the Bible.

When you approach wolves in a true spirit of wanting to understand, you will leave more confused than enlightened. They will say a bunch of words, which you will genuinely try to apply to normal life, but feel like a failure as you walk away. "They've done their best to explain," you think, "but I just don't get it." No light will dawn.

Now that many are confused, the wolves can more easily begin separating the fold. To isolate the sheep, a wolf might describe certain individuals or groups of people in a way that sounds like a smudged caricature and encourage separation from every other group besides the one under the wolf's control. Regardless of your depth of experience with the person (or group), this description may leave you with an uneasy feeling that, somehow, you have missed a major flaw in that person's character. No one likes to be taken for a fool—and wolves are both plausible and convincing. "Well, maybe I missed something," you find yourself thinking, or "Maybe I'd better avoid them." Surely—surely this worthy leader can't be wrong in describing a rival as a heretic, or a group of fellow saints as "schismatics." The language is a little strong, but—maybe that other group is really bad?

The confused can be easily misled and isolated. And it isn't just those who are less righteous. Sometimes righteous people greatly assist Satan's well-organized forces by becoming self-righteous, or distracted, or weary of being the good people that get spat on. Sometimes they want everything to turn out well so they don't have to admit an error in judgment.

Chaos Creation

Is there a difference between a schismatic, a devotee of division, and a wolf? Not much, if they are encouraging brokenness intentionally.

They do this through creating chaos, using the mosquito method of argumentation, and resolving conflicts with a "kill or cure."

- Chaos creates opportunity: Some wolves enjoy dropping a hornet's nest and scampering off. They'll pick off the weak of the herd at their leisure.

- Mosquito method of argumentation: Some wolves persistently drive opponents to distraction with needle-fine distinctions and definitions that normal believers couldn't care less about.

- Kill-or-cure conflict resolution: Either someone dies, or they win, or both. Nobody gets to walk away as friends.

Like Father (Satan), Like Child

*"Your adversary the devil prowls around like a
roaring lion, seeking someone to devour."*
—I Peter 5:8

A real, dyed-in-the-wool destroyer does not want to change
or acquiesce to anyone other than the god of self. The original
predator (Satan) made it his business to seek out the weaker
link and establish a connection in the Garden of Eden through
the medium of reasonable speech. He asked a Socratic-style
question[7] to remove Eve's defenses and implant seeds of doubt
before moving in for the kill.

- *"Did God actually say, 'You shall not eat of any tree in
  the garden'?"* (Genesis 3:1). The message is that God
  is a liar who doesn't say what He means. You have to
  read between the lines, which makes you clever and
  sophisticated.

- *"You will not surely die"* (Genesis 3:4), meaning
  disobedience will benefit rather than harm. He gets
  one to believe God doesn't want the best for you.

- *"You will be like God, knowing good and evil"* (Genesis
  3:5). This implies that God fears your power, so
  you have to go in and take it because He's guarding
  something He doesn't want you to have. Really God
  was guarding them from death, but Satan made
  disobedience sound like the common good of man.

---

[7]   He tried a similar style on the Lord regarding Job's state of faith—for example,
    "Does Job fear God for no reason?" (Job 1:9)—so I see this as a pattern.

69

- *"For God knows that when you eat of it your eyes will be opened"* (Genesis 3:5). God is a selfish tyrant who wants to keep you in bondage; that's why He's keeping back this ultimate good for Himself. That's how Satan sees his Creator, and that's how he wants to infect man to see God—and die.

Before we start blaming our ancestral parents, it's good to recognize that none of us would have made a different decision than that of Adam and Eve. Those same inclinations must be rooted out over a lifetime because of Satan's deceitful lies.

The worship of man,[8] fueled by Satan's deception, is the oldest and worst rebellion against God that unleashed His wrath and promoted our suffering. It's not surprising that wolves always produce a *lite* version of this particular error.

If Satan always appeared with red horns and a forked tail, holding a pitchfork, identification would be a simple process. Unfortunately, he almost always prefers showing up as a rather handsome and soft-spoken gentleman. My vision is that he likes wearing grey—playing for both sides, so to speak. His normal is scary, so he's always toned down until he's gotten what he wants and you're trapped.

It's hard to break the habit of listening to someone who is intelligent, persuasive, convincing, and completely assured of his own message. Satan is self-deluded and walks in the footprints of death. So do his followers.

---

[8]   "If the Divine call does not make us better, it will make us very much worse. Of all bad men religious bad men are the worst. Of all created beings the wickedest is one who originally stood in the immediate presence of God." C.S. Lewis, *Reflections on the Psalms*, 147

THE GENDER-NEUTRAL
TOOLS OF EVIL

In *People of the Lie,* author Scott Peck describes evil as "'live' spelled backwards,"[9] and abusive wolves act in this backwards fashion. They promote death by turning living, thinking humans into zombies overtaken by the desire to consume and destroy. Death is usually depicted as a gender-neutral being because it levels the playing field of life. (Another good fictional illustration is the sexless brain IT in Madeleine L'Engle's *Wind in the Door.*)

Scott Peck goes on to relay the difficulty of differentiation when he says, "It is hard to determine the sex of a snake."[10] Satan is not gender-centric in his choice of tools. He will use gossip and manipulation, as well as domination tactics, to achieve destruction of a person or group, and he hates the followers of Christ more than any other group. He can encourage self-centered thinking while sowing slow-growing seeds of compromise until survival becomes an idol (this is especially apparent in smaller churches). He can encourage talking about symptoms rather than dealing with root causes of evil.

Evil can appear ordinary, like the continual refusal to acknowledge personal failure or a need to be helped while

---

[9]   Peck, *People of the* Lie, 42.
[10] Peck, *People of the Lie,* 12.

emphatically insisting that everyone else has a problem. Evil is lazy and greedy, withering everything it touches. In the presence of evil, the mind can sometimes grind to a halt like an overworked machine, trying to separate so many threads of misinformation and false trails. "The evil are 'the people of the lie,' deceiving others as they also build layer upon layer of self-deception."[11]

Maybe the reason why Satan is described as a roaring lion is because he apes God (Martin Luther: "For where God built a church, there the devil would also build a chapel. Thus is the Devil ever God's ape").[12] Predators fear larger, stronger predators. The good news, as per C.S. Lewis in *That Hideous Strength*, is that Satan and his minions don't have an issue with destroying the tools they use; once the tools' usefulness is at an end, they will be destroyed.[13] Their masters hate their servants.

False Neutrality: A Tool for Evil

When you're dealing with wolves, remember that you're not just dealing with fallible but lovable human beings. You need to take sides, as there really is no spiritual Switzerland (neutral zone). The horror of warfare is that it is both impersonal and personal.

Anyone who is not on the side of Christ and His righteousness is automatically supporting, aiding, abetting, or participating in

---

[11] Peck, *People of the Lie*, 66.
[12] Barbour Publishing, *Heroes of the Faith: Memorable Quotes from Men and Women of Faith*, (Ohio: Barbour, 1998), 105.
[13] "In fighting those who serve devils one always has this on one's side; their Masters hate them as much as they hate us. The moment we disable the human pawns enough to make them useless to Hell, their own Masters finish the work for us. They break their tools." 314

the growth of evil as epitomized by Satan. The wolf is a pawn, a servant of sin, though a willing one.

Confusion: A Tool for Evil

One of the reasons Job and his friends spend many chapters debating, back and forth, about God and man and righteousness and wickedness—all based on their own observations—is because evil is a repellant, exhausting puzzle. If you have ever tried to separate wheat from tares by hand, it's a time-consuming process.

It's not always easy to see when people are confused, or when they intend to cause confusion in others. Intent is hard to prove, but the end result of unresolved confusion is isolation, destruction, and chaos. This reflects the Prince of Darkness, not the Prince of Peace.

Time: A Problem for Evil

Evil knows that it's on a short leash, and that eventual consequence is a source of terror. In Mark 5, we have a description of evil spirits begging Jesus to be allowed to destroy a herd of pigs—and the townspeople begging Jesus to leave. They were shaken to their core, knowing that Someone had the power both to heal a demon-possessed man and to send pigs to destruction.

Satan knows quite well that his time is limited. He's trying to make the most of it before he will have to submit to the light of Christ and spend eternity chained.

Despair: A Tool for Evil

Satan is a fan of despair. He will help people become ineffective in their faith and reluctant to scrub out festering wounds so they can get real healing: "Why try, if everything ends in disaster?"

In *The Silver Chair*,[14] C.S. Lewis describes a method of lulling victims into a false sense of security, into a heavy frame of mind. The victims of a spell tell themselves that it would be easier to give up and give over, to admit that everything is useless. Even on the brink of defeat, evil still fights to the death, hoping to regain the ground that it has lost. It tries to convince the people it has drawn into despair that it retains the power of life and death even after it's been thrown out.

Some fiery trials are masked as hopeless projects or grey piles of ash. The trials look like endless strings of petty complaints, purposeless lies, and continual accusations. These are the markers of pride rooted in the desire for autonomy. It's a constant "I'm rubber; you're glue" merry-go-round.

Self-Protection: A Potential Tool for Evil

Sometimes, you may be dealing with the residual effect of evil rather than the current reality. Victims of wolves, convinced that they must protect themselves at all costs, may become unexploded bombs of fear and anxiety if they refuse to accept the healing power of Christ. Some of Satan's victims were thrown to the ground before the evil spirit actually departed (presumably in a rage at having to concede defeat).

---

[14] C. S. Lewis, *The Silver Chair* (New York: Harper Collins, 1994), 79.

At the threat of another disruption, sometimes people grasp at retention before running or crawling away from danger. They desire the prized intangible form of security, whether they define it as peace and safety (or unity), and they will do anything for "it." They may go back into a diseased or burning house to get "it," or they will freeze like frogs in a boiling pot and refuse to move.

Satan does not care if believers destroy themselves through lack of activity, the idol of security, or through running away to nurse dreams of revenge. Whether his encouragement is to dwell on current circumstances or past history, Satan encourages people to become perpetual victims, always alert against someone who will let them down or remove valued possessions. Again, in the words of C.S. Lewis from the *Magician's Nephew,* he is "terribly practical"[15] in the sense that he is uninterested in anyone or anything that he cannot use.

> Fighting for survival is not necessarily a tool of good

Fighting for survival is not necessarily a tool of good.

Group Huddle: A Potential Tool for Evil

This shock of humankind being exposed for their natural evil is especially evident in organizations and groups where evil is almost a requirement for survival.

While he wasn't right about everything, Peck did make a good point in saying that specialization leads to "fragmentation of conscience,"[16] which in turn leads to a great opportunity for evil.

---

[15] C. S. Lewis, *The Magician's Nephew* (New York: Harper Collins, 1994), 79.

[16] Peck, *People of the Lie*, 217. This same section offers an example of Peck's questions on the morality of warfare and weaponry shifted from one department to another (ordnance to policy to White House).

If you don't know whom to blame, the responsible party is never found, and justice is never meted out.

Whenever the roles of individuals within a group become specialized, it becomes both possible and easy for the individual to pass the moral buck to some other part of the group. In this way, not only does the individual forsake his conscience but the conscience of the group as a whole can become so fragmented and diluted as to be nonexistent.[17]

Responsibility can be endlessly avoided under these headings:

- Unfamiliarity: Lack of technical knowledge about the subject matter

- Experiential biases: Requiring others to "walk a mile in *our* shoes"

- Personal exemption: Claiming that they, their friend, or their child has needs or wounds that make them special and unique

- Global experience: Thinking that anyone would retain the same type of meaning that they took from the experience

- Blame-shifting: Calling anyone who challenges their worldview petty/prideful/divisive/pharisaical, etc.

- Comparison and competition: Pointing out that others are worse than they are

- Self-affirmation loop: Believing that their group is uniquely right and superior because they have survived and all other groups are envious, wimpy, or wrong in their approach

---

[17]   Peck, *People of the Lie*, 218.

Group evil can be enhanced by shifting perspective from being for God to being against something: Satan, permissive church life, lack of discipline, particular worship style, etc. By focusing continually on something that is wicked rather than focusing on what is good and true and righteous altogether, tunnel vision can turn sheep into casualties of war.

Hope: The Antidote to Evil

To remain a hopeful Christian, you must read from those who have fought against wolves and won with the right spirit and the appropriate methods. Despite his checkered early years, Saint Augustine (referenced by both Protestants and Catholics alike) is counted as a church leader who successfully battled heresies and hoaxes throughout his long life. One of his works, *The City of God Against the Pagans*, can still be found as primary textual material in the religion and politics departments of Princeton. On his deathbed, it is said that Augustine of Hippo supplied directives for fighting invading hordes of barbarian Vandals.

For more modern examples, the "Prince of Preachers," Charles Spurgeon, would serve as the picture of a pastor who led a large flock without indulging in destructive tendencies. For a more modern martyr, Dietrich Bonhoeffer—murdered at the Flossenburg concentration camp by special order of Nazi leader Heinrich Himmler—would also do. Both of these men struggled with depression but promoted joy, long before John Piper coined the term "Christian hedonism."

While many other influencers could be mentioned, such as C.S. Lewis and J.R.R. Tolkien, their works could be considered supplemental rather than primary. They affirm that we are not alone in the fight, but the spiritual Marines on the front lines would be shepherds: pastors, teachers, and ordained men directly given care over their flocks.

SIGNS OF MANIPULATION

A wolf sees every normal response that indicates concern beyond self or overlooking a fault as a weak spot to exploit. Wolves consider love as equal to weakness, so they search out consistently loving, caring, kind people to use and abuse. That's why it's possible to find amazingly resilient, humane souls corralled near a wolf or cult leader. (Wolves often become cult leaders, feeding off the power that comes from establishing ultimate control over people's lives.)

If a wolf comes to you in a seemingly piteous state—fur bedraggled, look of pleading in the eyes—it's not a genuine call for help. It's a calculated move designed to bring your heart to the surface. If you refuse to help, the wolf may take the direct approach. You may be labeled all sorts of discouraging things that will add up to an assertion like this: "You're not caring enough, you're not loving, and this is what's wrong with the church today."

Perhaps you defend yourself and say, "I'm supposed to be a good steward, and I don't see from your history that you would be a good candidate for charity." Either there will be a generically true appeal that "people can change," or a veiled command: "You shouldn't hold the past over peoples' heads." While the future isn't required to mirror the past, a changed future includes a changed present. If no changes are made in the present, nothing will be different down the road.

It has been said (some say by Aristotle) that the difference between "genius" and "crazy" is a thin line. Likewise, the line of separation can seem equally thin between a zealous, strong-minded believer, a strong and original personality, and someone who manufactures harm for his own benefit.

When in doubt about someone's motivations, these are good discernment questions to ask about a person's life fruit: Who benefits from this person's behavior? Is he accountable to anyone other than a family member or sympathetic friend?

Satan's Lies: Doubt and Deceit

"Did God actually say, 'You shall not eat of any tree in the garden'?"
—*Genesis 3:1*

When doubt brings forth fruit, it is always bitter and accusatory. Satan may use the wolves' apparent victory as a means to whisper, "God doesn't care." Just like everything else that he whispers, his purpose is to destroy, but it can be a very effective seed of doubt.

Doubt is different from caution. A cautionary warning bell may mean you are not sure that God supports a circumstance or a person, but it does not necessarily mean you doubt God or His purposes. We are told to examine our own and others' motives as fruit inspectors. But we are never called to cynically question or openly cast doubt on God's motives, purposes, will, or character; this would be as insulting as Simon Magus trying to buy the gift of the Holy Spirit (Acts 8:18).

So don't let the lawless behavior of wolves turn you cold against your Lord (Matthew 24:12 –13). Doing so has made the lives of many believers powerless and ineffective. While wolves only have the power of deception, it is possible to allow them power over your life by focusing on the wrongs they have done to you. Perhaps the enemy has won a battle in your case or possibly captured your entire family line. Regardless, you must hold true to the hope offered in the Word.

By breaking the thread of deception, you—and possibly your family as well—can be freed from chains.

Personal Example

I once had an interaction with a person who wanted to secure my support for winning back his spouse. When we met in a public place, he was wearing dark glasses, which he'd never done before. After about 20 minutes of conversation, where he gave the impression that he was being calm and reasonable and taking a bad blow really well, he took off the glasses. His eyelids were red, and it was clear that he had been crying. Then he relayed a story through voicemail (an appeal to a third party of sorts), which explained some of the storm of emotion: his children had left him a voicemail asking him why he had engaged in destructive and hurtful behavior and broken his word. Through his tears, which seemed very genuine and heart-wrenching—especially given the awful circumstances—he glanced up for a moment. It was a calculating gleam; it was cold, inhuman, and certainly self-centered.

In that second, like a light bulb flicking on in my head, my inner misgivings about the scene became clear. For an hour, I had listened and tried to be empathetic, but a faint warning bell suddenly rang with startling clarity. As far as I know, I did not give any outward indication to show that the game was up. He had been laying a trail of breadcrumbs all throughout our conversation, about how the spouse was making a mistake in refusing to concede to his requests. As the persuasive tactics increased, it seemed clear that I was being recruited to be part of the convincing act and appeal to the spouse to backtrack on a deep conviction.

In the middle of trying to secure my support for relationship restoration, the wolf related another personal interaction and how it had not gone well. He tried to virtue-signal as a repentant person, but it did not sound like genuine sorrow. It was a subtle reminder that he would resent, forever, anything that I said that didn't match his preconceived estimation of support or encouragement.

Bear in mind, he was the guilty party. In another age, he probably would have died for his actions. One person courageously told him directly that he had taken every possible second chance and blown it like a stack of change at a slot machine, and his spouse had every right to walk away. At the exact same moment when he was asking for help, he was also trying to assert his right to my help, as though he owned it. He tried to pass off this manipulative move as being the bigger person, or taking his lumps like a man—"I didn't rip this person a new one like I would have before"—but it was just another performance in a long string of performances.

Once the hints had escalated to a crescendo, I asked a simple question: Was it in the spouse's best interests to change her mind? He went back to sniffling and quietly (noncommittally) indicated that maybe it wasn't, so I terminated the conversation as quickly as possible. There were tears in my eyes as I walked through the parking lot, but they were not for the wolf; they were for the children who would have to go through the painful life experience of finding out that their beloved playful father had a second and very dark personality. It's hard not to buy the convincing piteous act; it helped that this particular wolf had already shown his true colors.

If a wolf's guard is down, you may catch him revealing an incredibly petty, dreary, child-on-the-playground type of resentment. It will strike a jarring note with the overall act or façade that's often shown, of a sophisticated or beyond-reproach person of character who rises above small and petty things.

Wolves love to look grand and imposing, which is exactly how they hope to appear to others. (C.S. Lewis's depiction of Uncle Andrew in *The Magician's Nephew* is particularly on point here.)

The Alpha Wolf's Manipulation

"I know that after my departure fierce wolves will come in among you, not sparing the flock; and from among your own selves will arise men speaking twisted things, to draw away the disciples after them."

— *Acts 20:29–30*

The Alpha and the Charismatic Wolf may be hard to distinguish from each other, because both are struggling for top position but each one has a different skillset. If an Alpha and a Charismatic Wolf are joined in matrimony, they can be wretchedly effective as cult leaders. One can charm while the other strikes.

Most wolves in an alpha position have an element of attraction, whether or not it is charismatic. The alpha may use impressive communication skills to form connections and draw others to himself, manipulating through words. He may use some type of attraction beyond charm, something that excites admiration such as force of will or an impressive array of esoteric knowledge (or brute force). He may be so passionate about a vision or a goal that the strength of the conviction replaces charisma. Conviction has a drawing power beyond personality.

Some alphas are outwardly unimpressive in speech and person; while fueled by a vision or goal, their real strength lies in conviction rather than charisma. They are fully convinced they have what the world needs; some of the world will become convinced that this person can provide such a thing. The mannerisms may be off-putting—such as a monotone voice accompanying a wildly speculative theology—but it's rather like finding an obsessive clean freak with a string of messy divorces or a wedding planner with a string of broken engagements. Clearly, the outward man does not reflect the inward drive.

As with Absalom, the son of King David, a Charismatic Wolf can charm his way into men's hearts with ease. Perhaps he has a bold and dashing style that appeals to fighters. Maybe he has the ability to pry secrets out of near strangers, allowing them to divulge long-held secrets by the appearance of a sympathetic ear.

The Communicator Wolf's Manipulation

"He shall seduce with flattery those who violate the covenant, but the people who know their God shall stand firm and take action."

— *Daniel 11:32*

If the wolf is in the pulpit, he may preach on charity and sacrificial love (or endless sermons of judgment from Jude), perhaps with pointed looks. The congregation may not know the motivation for this sudden desire for topical sermons, but you know and he knows the reason for the sudden inspiration. If challenged, the Preacher Wolf will have some good surface answer couched in vague terms, such as, "I just felt moved by the Spirit on this topic," or "I was reading through II Corinthians 8, and it was impressed upon me that our congregation would really benefit from this reminder." Maybe he will use a more aggressive and accusatory tone and hint at a level of secret ministerial knowledge: "It's become necessary to address persistent habits of lack of charity and goodwill." Oh, the power plays.

Some popular communicators[18] have a personal history of breakups or church splintering that belies their strong words about faith, virtue, and self-control. Their personal habits of faith and godliness move them in steady succession to smaller and more controlled groups without every rejoining the larger invisible church. First comes isolation, then comes suspicion of every other Christian branch (that is never pure enough), then comes the eventual splintering of that group that is forced to start all over.

Watch out for leaders and communicators whose trail is littered with confusion, chaos, tension, and arguments. Every church they enter breaks up. Every small group that begins well ends in fights and tears. There is continual unease until they leave. Once they leave, everyone feels like celebrating.

Sometimes people really can talk "damned nonsense," as described by C.S. Lewis in *Mere Christianity*.[19] A normal person's assumption is that communication is meant for illumination, for light, for discovery. If communication is used for destruction, the strategy is to wrap people round and round in layers of conflicting messages until a weak spot appears, and the snake strikes.

---

[18] The *communicator* label can be applied to an ordained church leader (pastor, elder, deacon), author of any media type on Biblical subjects (writer, podcaster, vlogger), or speaker on a stage. Since wolves are primarily identified as false *teachers*, they need a communication platform of some sort to transfer their ideas.

[19] C. S. Lewis, *Mere Christianity* (New York: MacMillan, 1965), 31.

Wolf-in-Training's Manipulation

"And my servant Job shall pray for you, for I will accept his prayer not to deal with you according to your folly."

—Job 42:8

Misery truly does love company, and controllers like to use those who are already isolated. The Wolf-in-Training is not quite an Alpha, and not yet an Influencer Wolf, but he may dream of holding an influential role. He may cultivate relationships with the spouse or the children of leaders, simply to be within a few steps of the powerful.

While there is no need to ostracize people who simply have solitary habits (or are shy), be wary of the person who never seems to really gel with the others ("set apart") unless they are directing the action. This extreme individual may have a method and purpose to pulling aside others on the fringes for long talks, or using social media to cultivate connections with small groups already "on the outs" with other believers. As shown by Absalom in the early stages of his coup (II Samuel 15), wolves know how to pick out the weak and vulnerable from among the flock.

If a church becomes marked with unease or there is animosity building between formerly good friends, sometimes it is valuable to ask, "When did *X* and *Y* get mad at each other?" There may be many interconnected roots, but you can often trace it back to one or two people sending out invasive shoots of gossip, intrigue, and veiled accusations. If the Wolf-in-Training is involved, you may be able to stop the friction before it escalates to a church fight. If the Wolf-in-Training has teamed up with an Influencer Wolf and a Leader Wolf, the situation may get very messy before it is resolved.

Think about Job's friends—an ancient example of the worst small group ever. They came to weep with someone who wept, they tried to address the root cause of Job's weeping, and then they became an echo chamber of accusation. Against their friend, they became mired in conflict, a diseased holy huddle. If God had not decided to administer discipline, they might have turned into self-righteous wolves, parading their ignorant assumptions as truth.

Influencer Wolf's Manipulation

> *"The prince of the power of the air, the spirit that is now at work in the sons of disobedience."*
>
> *—Ephesians 2:2*

An Influencer Wolf is often female. She will give the impression of having no agenda while getting information from you: this person believes that information equates to the power of influence. Once the "information stick" is in her capable hands, the Influencer Wolf will use it until you wish you'd never confided in her.

Rather like a spider, the Influencer Wolf will weave webs to ensnare, using the power of the spoken word to create division, strife, and false unity. This type of wolf seems to work alone while paving the way for the other wolves to set up camp in the middle of a sheepfold. It's a tricky double-agent job.

The first step will be the exchange of personal information, business networking, or the relation of a heart-wrenching tragedy (her own or another's). The initial topic will be something innocuous, designed to relax your guard.

The second step will be an appeal to the value of the topic of interest and the steady, seductive pull toward (a) impassioned debate, (b) drawing out of personal history, (c) gossip about others' failings, (d) encouragement toward fear and doubt (with lip service to the idea that fear and doubt are bad or debilitating), or (e) appealing to one's Savior complex ("only you/this group can address this particular need").

All of this is so much eyewash, but it's very effective for many reasons. One, the Influencer Wolf gains power from being close to the Leader Wolf; in the role of advisor and confidante, the Influencer is given tidbits of information while others guess. Influencers revel in the dissemination of information with the cards close to their chest—know when to hold 'em, know when to fold 'em is the game. Walking or running is beneath an Influencer's dignity.

The Influencer doesn't want to be at the top, only within spitting distance. Her Achilles' heel is the loss of the ear of the leadership. Every Leader Wolf must be replaced once his power wanes, as he becomes too sick or old to wield power effectively. If the Influencer Wolf feels that no one is listening to her—or worse that people are laughing at her (mockery)—she may decide in a shrewd kind of calculating wisdom to pack up and move on to another host group.

You will know that the Influencer Wolves are flexing their muscles and preparing to clear the way for others to enter when they start dropping hints. Nothing aggressive at first, just a few threads thrown here or there.

- Someone interesting is coming into town, so let's go listen to them speak.

- We've just listened to a wonderful sermon series on a new (obscure) theory—let's meet and discuss.

- Let's connect at a cultural event (science fair, book fair, music club, book club, local art display) and have a meaningful experience involving a neutral enjoyable third object (food, wine, song, dance).

- An old connection is in town; we should connect and just let the past be the past (i.e., bury the hatchet and just ignore the fact that the old connection never apologized for bad behavior).

Influencer Wolves gather power as either creators or destroyers of relationships, either by bringing people together or splitting them up. If sowing seeds is meant to bear fruit (thorns or otherwise), this wolf will work the ground and remove any obstacles that would impede progress. If splitting is in view, the Influencer Wolves will sow seeds of doubt about the intentions and motivations of the other side and will do their best to paint these others in a dark and horrible light.

The human shields who protect the Influencer Wolves from becoming known are those either in thrall to them, or the kind and tenderhearted who spent time helping with issues of life (loneliness, anxiety, etc.). Most of us want to see that something can be redeemed or gleaned even from bad history (the return on investment versus the sunk cost principle). The human shield provides an air of normalcy and sanity to an otherwise crazy setup.

The Influencer Wolf doesn't hang out with the Loner Wolf, who tends to bring a downer element to the party, and usually intrudes with problems that do not cater to the Influencer's taste.

Loner Wolf's Manipulation

> *"Whoever isolates himself seeks his own desire; he breaks out against all sound judgment."*
>
> —*Proverbs 18:1*

Like Gollum in Tolkien's *Lord of the Rings* series, the Loner Wolf seems to be lost in a cloud of internal conflict. Frequently in discouragement, most likely troubled by some sort of habit of excess (drugs, alcohol, porn), this person can be very well-versed in the latest psychological terms and methods. Yet talking about recovery never seems to bring about any real healing because the Loner Wolf always deals with the same personal issues.

With a tendency to hang out at the extreme end of anti-authority sentiment, this wolf will often get drawn into a cult group because of its counter-cultural or unique blend. Like a rolling stone, he will have trouble staying in one place for long. The Loner Wolf will tend to get in the leader's way but can't be forcibly removed; there is no collateral to hold in reserve or remove, no family member slavishly dedicated to the cause.

If the pack is ever accused of being unloving and uncaring, the Loner Wolf can be useful as a great cover story, a shield against criticism. "Well, look at George," they might say. "We've tirelessly taken care of him, and boy, does he have issues!" The contrast is noticeable because the pack's intense methods and perspectives seem to discourage George's level and method of participation. George's friends are usually as unkempt as he is, but they do not stay long.

The Loner Wolf's more bizarre behavior can always be excused because he is always on the brink of either being kicked out or slinking off to another group. He will be welcomed in the sheep's fold until he disappears and returns to his true home—carrying all sorts of useful information into the cave. The other wolves will sniff him over and log the information, accepting him as the go-between scout, and the dysfunctional cycle begins all over again. It satisfies the Loner Wolf's twisted sense of normalcy to be always on the brink of removal from fellowship with his true pack. Both parties benefit from the interaction.

It is not a kindness for a genuine congregation to repeatedly accept the Loner Wolf and hope for a change that doesn't happen, any more than it's a kindness to allow an Influencer or a Leader Wolf to come in and follow the dark side of their natures. It doesn't help any congregation work through issues of love, sanctification, or encouragement. It only helps both groups to become worse, after the wolves have planted their seeds of doubt and distress.

DISCERNMENT

K nowing a wolf's true nature, the tools, and the signs they
use can help you identify a wolf. You will need to separate
truth from lies, aggressive sheep from wolves, and real repentance
from remorse.

In keeping with the principle of starting with self-examination,
we can start with self-induced lies. Next, we can move on to the
separation of truth from half-truths (or complete lies), as an aid to
discerning a wolf from a sheep.

Self-Justification: Lies You Tell Yourself about Wolves

Sometimes you impair your own ability to discern. Red flags and
instincts can serve you well, but if you are already involved with a
wolf, the habit of self-justification is strong. It's especially hard to
see through a lie when it's paired with a half-truth.

This is a short list of the ways I have fooled myself with these half-truths in the past, about someone whom I now consider a wolf. The types of self-justification do not differ much between personal life and church life situations.

Self-Justification: Half-Truth	Real Truth
Playing it safe hasn't worked. I'll team up with a messy person, and we'll both reach our goals.	The messy person remains messy and no one reaches goals.
Chasing family approval is useless, and they just don't like anyone I date. (He was 35 years my senior.)	Your family will like someone who actually fits in, which is better than demanding the family accept the wolf.
My significant other started going to church because of me, so God must be working in his heart.	Missionary dating success stories are a rare exception, rather than the rule—and not approved in Scripture (II Corinthians 6:14).
I can't escape feeling trapped in the circumstances of my life, so I'll pour time and energy into this frog, and he will become a prince.	Investment doesn't guarantee result. Planting a gold talent in the ground doesn't mean it will produce a crop of money (Matthew 25:18).
This person appeared, so God wants me to be involved in his life.	In Matthew 4, Satan appeared to tempt, not to be involved.

Self-Justification: Half-Truth	Real Truth
All service to God is good service.	Legalism masking as holy living. Nadab and Abihu died for the assumption that God would bless any service they offered.
You only live once, so jump off that cliff in faith!	False bravado masking despair. Also, something Satan told Jesus to do (Matthew 4:6).
Why not try this? Everything else has failed anyway.	Fatalism masking despair. I wasn't asking *why* "everything" had failed.
I'm in too deep to back out.	I failed to ask for help out of the pit that I had dug for myself.

A particular type of pride and arrogance leads enabling sheep to say to themselves, out of pity or a desire to be influencers, "**I** can heal this person. **I** know exactly what they need; **I've** been in their situation before. They can really benefit from **my** experience and wisdom." The only person who really heals is Christ, through the power of the Holy Spirit. God provides, and man is allowed to carry the baskets of fragments left over (Mark 8:19).

Truth from Lies

> *"The scribes and the Pharisees sit on Moses' seat, so do and observe
> whatever they tell you, but not the works they do. For they preach,
> but do not practice. They tie up heavy burdens, hard to bear, and lay
> them on people's shoulders, but they themselves are not willing to move
> them with their finger. They do all their deeds to be seen by others."*
>
> —*Matthew 23:2–5*

As indicated in I and II and III John, there is a stark difference between truth and lies. (Our culture likes to sit on a fence halfway and proclaim that everyone has a handle on "their" version of a truth perspective, and this simply is not scriptural.) Truth is sometimes searingly honest and requires change; it can be a scalpel that divides bone from sinew. A half-truth creates a lot of frustration as you try to work out what it really means, as it is hard to distinguish from the speaker's real agenda. A real truth is offered to the listener's benefit and has worldwide applicability beyond the current time and place. A half-truth can feel like a searing spear of insight (more accurately portrayed as an emotional sucker punch) but is ultimately empty when scrutinized.

In Matthew 23, Jesus says that it's possible to implement even the Pharisees' official advice without mirroring their habits. Many speakers and authors can be insightful in one or two areas. Some outright heretics can make quite practical points. Not every one of a communicator's thoughts or ideas need to be off base for them to be tagged as a divisive person, or someone who spreads Biblical misinformation. C.S. Lewis said something similar in *Mere Christianity*, that belief as a Christian doesn't mean that "all the other religions are simply wrong all through."[20] In a state of

---

[20]   Lewis, *Mere Christianity*, 29.

discernment, you can affirm specific areas of agreement without affirming the nature of the communicator as true and correct.

Jesus drew a stark line of comparison between the Pharisees' words offered for effect and heart-based service. In a similar way, you may be able to observe that when wolves are in leadership, their actions won't match their official positions. Maybe their character seems to shift, chameleon-like, depending on who they hang around; this two-faced behavior always lies at the back of your mind. Perhaps they offer calculated flattery (or insults), and their real motivations seem to be a mystery.

As a sheep, it's important to be aware of your own reactions, as these reactions can quietly detect liars. Maybe you are always slightly restless in their company, longing to be outside, breathing fresh air. You may become tongue-tied in their presence, either because they are so combative or because their version of being reasonable is somewhat terrifying. Even if you possess a strong will and principles, you may find yourself unaccountably wishing to just run away—from them, from the situation, from any involvement. Over time, you'll become more guarded and wary the longer you know them.

Also, when you compare notes with others (to see if you're going crazy), the versions will not add up. It's not a difference of perspective with underlying unity, like "The gospel of Mark emphasizes time, but the gospel of John emphasizes the Word"; the accounts differ significantly, causing you to doubt whether or not you know the person truly.

Aggressive Sheep from Wolf

"Blessed are the peacemakers."
—Matthew 5:9

Diligently examine the fruits of those who appear to be wolves. There is always a possibility of misidentification. Woe to the person who identifies an actual brother or sister in Christ as an enemy, simply due to personality conflict or difference in vision.

This is a deeper dive into the who part of the puzzle—because sometimes aggressive sheep or lead sheep can be mistaken for actual predators. It can be hard to discern whether the person is a wolf, just some hothead, or a confrontational brother. How can you be sure that you're dealing with a true wolf?

Some sheep are quite self-centered, somewhat manipulative, a little two-faced, and some have colossal tempers. Thus, it can be hard to distinguish between marks of indwelling or persistent sin and walking in a habit of intentional sin.

For instance, Jesus had things to say to the Sons of Thunder (Luke 9:55), who wanted to apply payback to the Samaritans rejecting Jesus. In contrast to wolves, the Sons of Thunder accepted Jesus's rebuke and applied His methods.

Sometimes it helps to see a side-by-side comparison, especially if you are more tempted to light fires than create peace.

Ravenous Wolf	Aggressive Sheep
Never takes responsibility for destruction/bad effect on others (Lamech in Genesis 4, boasting of murder in response to an insult)	Will apologize or repent eventually (Jacob repaying Esau part of the lost inheritance in Genesis 32–33)

Ravenous Wolf	Aggressive Sheep
Manic dedication to self/the cause	Serves Christ but in a self-centered way
The sheep engage in fascinated hero-worship or repulsion. The wolf engages in victim-blaming of those repulsed	Those repulsed by the aggressive sheep can communicate their feelings/impressions to the sheep, who then will try to change
Destruction follows in his wake—the spiritual equivalent of burnt-out buildings	Frustration and discouragement follow in his wake, but people's lives/faith are retained (holding on to truth with difficulty)
Not submissive—tries to be the authority in any situation (Korah, Dathan, and Abiram in Numbers 16)	Not submissive in conflict with others, but will grudgingly obey ruling authorities (Miriam and Aaron in Numbers 12)
Presents a disarming front to the world	Isn't interested in appearances
Does good deeds to be seen and applauded (miffed if not "recognized")	Does good deeds without calling attention to them—as a part of life
Lives in an altered state (fantasy)	Retains a hold on common sense

Ravenous Wolf	Aggressive Sheep
Seems to have a magical/ mystical hold over others while vilifying enemies	Is charismatic but has some enemies he'll try to love/work with
Full of anger, which followers see as justified	Struggles with anger but is open to a need to change
Expects to win every disagreement	Expects losses but tries hard to win
Every loss becomes an endless grievance	Can nurse grudges but can also let go
Obsessive, single-minded focus	Focused but has other interests
Cares about people as long as they contribute to the cause	Cares about people and the cause but essentially sees results as God's job

It's difficult to distinguish between a movement, a campaign, and just ordinary sinful strife between people. One of the markers of those who spread dissent is that an atmosphere of disruptive tension follows in their wake; even when peace has been accomplished, they want to stir things up. Dissent and controversy are in the air they breathe. It is unlikely that they could retain an identity without it.

This is different from the stirring that happens when sin is being addressed (which no one likes!) because the person who wants to gain a peaceful outcome will tend to offer his own life as a sacrifice. This was true for Moses and Aaron hitting the ground and pleading with God to save rather than to destroy. It was true for Jesus, and it was certainly true for Peter and Paul.

Repentance from Remorse

"Bear fruit in keeping with repentance."
—*Matthew 3:8*

Repentance is a major difference between a sheep and a wolf, but the signs can be hard to read. Is it a Judas move, melodramatically intoning the obvious (*"I have sinned by betraying innocent blood,"* Matthew 27:4) and then compounding sin by engaging in self-harm? Is it a David move, admitting sin and then naming one of his sons after the confronter (Nathan)? Does the apparently repentant one make any permanent life changes?

Real repentance shows up in action, not just in words. It sounds like Zacchaeus, who gladly donated all of his ill-gotten gains and paid more than the law required (Luke 19). Real repentance is evident in the life of the Apostle Paul, who turned from persecuting to accepting persecution for the sake of Christ, and out of love for the brethren.

Real repentance means a change in focus and direction. After repentance, the thing that used to matter ceases to have any real power or hold over that person. A previous liar will be passionate about the truth. A prior thief will be inspired to share with others (Ephesians 4:28). Former gossips and slanderers will

> Real repentance means a change in focus and direction

be passionately interested in speech that builds and edifies the hearer.

Wolves may admit in vague or generic terms to "sin" or "bad behavior," or they may pull out Paul's passage about *"Oh, wretched man that I am"* (Romans 7:24), complete with voice quiver. However, there will be a false note to this performance because they like secrecy. Unless the sin has already become known, they make historical admittance seem like heroism. Admittance of current or recent guilt is beyond hard; it's like pulling teeth while the dental patient tries to bite you. Wolves almost always try to pick their own punishment because they don't trust anyone else to be truly gracious, i.e., the opposite of themselves.

By contrast, the really repentant will have gone through all these steps:

- Confession: It has a dual purpose—to air the error in public, and to establish a basis point for change.

- Contrition: Repentant sinners are willing to listen to the pain they have caused others in a real way, without making any excuses or justifications. They bring it up as evidence against themselves later on, because it remains a tender point.

- Forgiveness: It is requested, not demanded.

- Oversight: They may recognize their need for others speaking into their lives and ask for accountability partners.

- Boundaries: They will limit themselves voluntarily because they know their own triggers, and they don't want to fall into the same error that caused so much pain.

- Gratitude: Remorseful people may go straight back to grumbling about consequences; repentant people will usually be glad for the boring old routine of life returning to normal, as it is better than the excitement of their old ways.

Having Done All, Stand Fast

While it's difficult to separate the strong-minded sheep from actual wolves, no amount of sheep's clothing can shield them forever. Rooting them out requires the tempered steel of a true leader, a servant of servants, to listen to the Spirit's still small voice that says, "Wait. Don't run. Stand your ground. Live out my Word in fear and trembling."

SECTION 3:
THE AFFECTED CONGREGATION

THE FEARING CONGREGATION: A TARGET FOR WOLVES

The examples throughout this chapter are based on the assertion that the Bible is the primary rule for faith and life, with the Old Testament as our clearest example of the early church. Consider the nation of Israel during their wandering years in the wilderness and when they were being established as a nation prior to King David's arrival. When they cried out to God, were they always being honest with their Father about what they wanted? Did their Father always meet or exceed their expectations?

Simply because a congregation experiences suffering does not mean that it is a completely innocent party. Sometimes, the congregation contributes to its situation, acting as its own worst enemy. Lack of internal unity, or resistance to God's express purpose, will make the flock an easy target.

While it's wrong to blame the innocent victim (e.g., Naboth in 1 Kings 21, who did nothing to earn Ahab's covetousness), it's just as wrong to avoid the necessary question: Did our sin make it easy for wolves to attack us?

Not everyone who cries out in pain or limps is a victim of a circumstance or a third party. Sometimes people can be victims of their own desires.

Victims or Rebels?

After God established Moses and Aaron, we are told about three wolves who arose in the midst of the camp: Korah, Dathan, and Abiram. Their rebellion led to their destruction (Numbers 16). But prior to their uprising, the entire nation was wracked with physical distress and endless fears that God would punish them with death in the wilderness. While they witnessed God destroy their enemies, they were not thankful for that deliverance or for their appointed leaders. They continually complained, fearing that the journey was purposeless. They hurled accusations at God. "Didn't we tell you to 'leave us alone' because service to the Egyptians was better than dying in the wilderness?" (*"Is it because there are no graves in Egypt?"* Exodus 14:11.)

Their complaints and fears were not logical—everyone dies in time—but they clearly had a perspective that the past was better than their present. I call it the "It would have been better" hindsight view. Better to postpone the inevitable (death) than to live under affliction meant for their sanctification. Better to have servitude to the world than service to God. Better, in fact, to die as slaves than die as free men.

For 40 years, the Israelites acted in constant fear and anxiety. Because they didn't trust that what He told them was true, all their fears became true.

Choosing Fear over Faith: A Self-Fulfilling Prophetic Loop

From Exodus to Deuteronomy, the early congregants alternately accuse God of wanting to kill them and then moan about how God's purpose is evil (e.g., the Egyptians could have just killed us back "home"). After many signs to the contrary (including manna), they cry about how God doesn't provide for their real needs. They weep about the lack of meat, so God sends quail and tells them their fulfilled desire will become a curse: eat until it comes out of your nose. Literally, the name of the place where they wail for meat (Kibroth-Hataavah) means "graves of craving" (Numbers 11).

They had begged God for freedom while in Egypt. Yet when He gave it to them, they did not know how to live as a free people. They avoid or reject God's decrees, as they fear everything and everyone *but* God—yet they expect blessing. They get fire instead (see the "Wolves on Fire" section below, on Numbers 15 and 16).

This dilemma mirrors their response to Moses, flexing his leadership muscles 40 years before he came to the rescue. (*"Who made you a prince and a judge over us?"* Exodus 2:14.) The fact that Moses himself had a lot to learn and unlearn is evident as well.

Complaint Is Not a Faith-Filled Response

I am not saying that silencing complaints is the answer to a complaining congregation. Sometimes complaints require conscientious investigation and real-time, practical answers. For instance, complaints led the Apostle Paul to address serious issues of incest in the Corinthian congregation (*"It is actually reported that there is sexual immorality among you, and of a kind that is not tolerated even among pagans, for a man has his father's wife"* I Corinthians 5:1–2). But questions repeated on a continual loop are different from questions leading to action. The repeat-question method is often just an attempt to control the conversation.

Sometimes telling people to "just stop" really is an answer. Stop complaining. Stop pointing out everyone else's flaws. Stop fearing—it will not help. To invoke a common saying, "When you find yourself in a hole, stop digging."

After their exodus from Egypt, the Israelites faced the unparted Red Sea. This was a real test, a crisis of faith, and they apparently said a lot about their fears. Moses provides the "just stop" answer to the congregation moaning about doom and destruction before the Egyptian army drowns. *"The Lord shall fight for you, and you have only to be silent"* (Exodus 14:14).

Moses further identifies the Israelites' real problem in year two of wandering in the Wilderness of Sin. After bitter water is turned sweet at Marah (meaning "bitterness"), they're already complaining about death by hunger. God offers manna, and Moses summarizes their problem against authority: *"Your grumbling is not against us but against the Lord"* (Exodus 16:8).

By the time the Israelites are facing another felt need (lack of water) at Rephidim (Exodus 17), they are ready to fight their appointed leader to the death. Moses is asking questions (*"Why do you quarrel with me? Why do you test the Lord?"*) without getting answers. The people are asking questions (*"Why did you bring us up out of Egypt, to kill us and our children and our livestock with thirst?"*), which aren't really questions so much as complaints on a repeated loop. But the Lord provided for them yet again when he gave water after Moses pleads *"They are almost ready to stone me."* Because of their constant questioning (i.e., complaints), the Scriptures say that the place was renamed Massah (meaning "testing") and Meribah (meaning "quarreling").

The response of the people implies that they do not want the answers that God has already provided. They have already experienced God's provision of water, food, and victory against enemies (including Egypt). Regardless of the answer, they grumble on.

A congregation mired in complaint is not a congregation living by the fruit of the Spirit: love, joy, peace, patience, kindness, goodness, faithfulness, gentleness, self-control. Some congregations really do act like nothing is their fault. They will complain about everything and take responsibility for nothing. This makes them a target for destruction, both from internal and external sources. Internally, lack of living by the fruit of the Spirit will lead to grumbling, and God will not tolerate continual grumbling. Externally, grumbling will leave a congregation vulnerable to predators who search for groups lacking unity and the shielding power of faith. A congregation that does not believe that God will protect it through suffering is a congregation suffering an internal crisis of faith. And none of these issues will help in fighting wolves.

This continual complaining is not the same as asking for help; when complaint turns to demand, that will elicit nearly the same response from our Parent as a toddler receives from throwing a tantrum. And this rejection of the Shepherd, from His methods to His leaders, invites predators. (Again, see the section "Wolves on Fire".)

Fear of Man versus Fear of God

> *"We are not able to go up against the people,*
> *for they are stronger than we are."*
>
> —Numbers 13:31

Group fear can also become fuel for rebellion against God.

In Numbers 13 and 14, rulers and representatives of each of the 12 tribes are chosen to spy out the land of Canaan, which God had promised to give as an inheritance to Israel. Good reports about Canaan are brought back by only two men: Caleb from Judah and Joshua from Ephraim. The other 10 spies sowed seeds of fear in the people, focusing on the difficulties of the task before them. The grapes are huge, but so are the people. The cities are fortified.

The Israelites declare their desire for a democratic overthrow of God's choice: *"Let us choose a leader and go back to Egypt"* (Numbers 14:4). In a similar fashion to a Jerusalem crowd's reaction to Jesus, Caleb and Joshua are threatened by an angry, stone-wielding mob for telling them to believe God's Word. Caleb and Joshua nearly die for their offer of good news that the people are well able to fight their enemies and inherit the Promised Land.

As a preventive measure against punishment, Moses "reminds" God of His purpose in bringing out the people from Egypt, but God reminds Moses that a temporary pardon does not mean the debt is wiped clean. *"None of the men who have seen my glory and my signs that I did in Egypt and in the wilderness, and yet have put me to the test these ten times and have not obeyed my voice, shall see the land that I swore to give to their fathers"* (Numbers 14:22–23). There are permanent consequences to repeatedly ignoring God's good advice, so the 10 spies die by plague. Instantly.

Family Trouble: Rejecting the Lord's Choices

In the second month of year two in the wilderness, two sons of Aaron offer "strange fire" before the Lord and die (Leviticus 10). They do this against the express wishes of God, who mandated a certain type of incense to be burned in His honor. These two priests had seen a Revelation-like vision of God standing on a *"pavement of sapphire stone, like the very heaven for clearness"* (Exodus 24:10), but the consequence of their unnecessary creativity was permanent.

Later on, the spirit of complaint infects Miriam and Aaron against their brother Moses, the Lord's anointed prophet (Numbers 12). Since these leaders show a lack of godly fear by speaking out against an appointed leader, God shows His displeasure by striking Miriam with leprosy. Miriam does recover, but it seems significant that she dies first out of the three siblings.

Despite the great sacrifices made in God's service, none of these three siblings were allowed to see the Promised Land. Service to God does not mean perpetual absolution from consequences.

> Service to God does not mean perpetual absolution from consequences

Nostalgia and Faux Repentance: A Wish to Avoid Suffering

> *"But they presumed to go up to the heights of the hill country, although neither the ark of the covenant of the Lord nor Moses departed out of the camp. Then the Amalekites and the Canaanites who lived in that hill country came down and defeated them and pursued them, even to Hormah."*
>
> —*Numbers 14:44–45*

By the third month of year two, Moses goes to receive word from the Lord out of a smoking, spitting, volcanic Mount Sinai. In a fit of nostalgia and fear of abandonment, the people ask Aaron to make gods for them. When Moses reappears, they drink the golden ashes and die from plague. The promise of judgment leads the people to a faux repentance: "We'll admit sin, we'll get back in God's good graces, and then we can go to the Promised Land!"

Basically, they mean "We will avoid all the pain, suffering, and consequences for persistent sin that the Lord has laid on us because we see no value in suffering." Moses fires back, *"Because you have turned back from following the Lord, the Lord will not be with you"* (Numbers 14:43).

Sometimes, losses happen because wolves are allowed to win temporarily. Sometimes, God's people earn their losses by ignoring His processes.

Contrast from Non-Israel: Experience and Heritage versus Faith and Trust

> *"When Jesus heard this, he marveled and said to those who followed him, 'Truly, I tell you, with no one in Israel have I found such faith. I tell you, many will come from east and west and recline at table with Abraham, Isaac, and Jacob in the kingdom of heaven, while the sons of the kingdom will be thrown into the outer darkness.'"*
>
> *—Matthew 8:10–12*

Jethro the Midianite, father of Moses's wife Zipporah, appears early in the Israelite journey across the desert. I see this intervention as one of God's early previews of the centurion (Matthew 8) and the Syrophoenician woman (Mark 7), showing that outsiders can sometimes be filled with faith, while native-born members of the flock can die of fear. (Sheep can die of fright.)

The fact that his daughter is having severe marital issues doesn't stop Jethro from traveling to meet his son-in-law to confirm the news about God's power and victory over Egypt. Does he demand that Zipporah be taken back, or challenge Moses to a duel? No, he voluntarily sacrifices to God as the Lord of lords. Jethro also offers Moses feedback on his exhausting routine of personally overseeing every single dispute. That feedback led to the creation of a judicial appointment system, allowing Moses to delegate disputes to judges appointed over increasingly large groups.

Jethro had neither seen Egyptian bodies wash up on shore nor eaten manna before he traveled. But in his visit to his son-in-law,

Jethro shows more faith in the invisible hand of God (and more trust in His appointed leader) than the people who had walked on dry land through walls of water.

It's useless to claim a heritage of faith if your everyday life is marked by fear of everything but God. Experience of God's providence or His blessings is not the same as faith.

However, the example of Jethro (and other non-Israelite believers) shows that redemption is realistically available for those who make errors in judgment, which can happen to anyone.

BUILDING A WOLF PACK (OR CULT)

"And seeing in the distance a fig tree in leaf, [Jesus] went to see if he could find anything on it. When he came to it, he found nothing but leaves, for it was not the season for figs. And he said to it, 'May no one ever eat fruit from you again.'"

—Mark 11:13, 14

If wolves are so great at destroying, how do they build a following?

- They primarily build a following around sheep, using their different nature as an attraction point.

- They attract other wolves by use of power and influence, using deluded sheep as shields.

- The penalty for leaving the group is death (spiritual, connective, or otherwise).

How do you trust your own judgment if you tend to fall for the wrong person's story? How do you spot the difference between a lone prophet like Jeremiah and a lone wolf like Ravi Zacharias?

Anthony Storr in *Feet of Clay* explains how to spot them:

> Gurus are isolated people, dependent upon their disciples, without the possibility of being disciplined by a church or criticized by contemporaries. They are above the law. The guru usurps the place of God. Whether gurus have suffered from manic-depressive illness, schizophrenia, or any other form of recognized, diagnosable mental illness is interesting but ultimately unimportant. What distinguishes gurus from more orthodox teachers is not their manic-depressive mood swings, not their thought disorders, not their delusional beliefs, not their hallucinatory visions, not their mystical state of ecstasy: it is their narcissism.[21]

While they are supremely self-focused, wolves assume a mantle of authority and confidence, which draws in the sheep. These qualities can be combined in either an openly ruthless leader or a charismatic leader; either way, humans are also social creatures, and we live and die in habits and patterns. Even if we want to avoid the company of others, like hermits, we will end up making connections.

---

[21]   Anthony Storr, *Feet of Clay: Saints, Sinners, and Madmen: A Study of Gurus* (The Free Press/Simon & Schuster, 1966) (quoted in Jon Krakauer's *Under the Banner of Heaven*, New York: Vintage Books, 2004), 199.

<u>Perpetuating Trouble</u>

> *"Remind them of these things, and charge them before God not to quarrel about words, which does no good, but only ruins the hearers . . . avoid irreverent babble, for it will lead people into more and more ungodliness, and their talk will spread like gangrene."*
>
> —II Timothy 2:14-17

If the wolf hasn't already created his own separate group, you can find him at the center of unease in the congregation he has joined. He will seek out other troublemakers until there is a group of people unsatisfied with the host congregation. At that point, they can easily create a cult.

The first stage of manufactured trouble may be whispering, which may lead to backbiting and certainly to gossip. Gossip is empty of purpose and only holds a negative value. It's a highly valued tool for the wolf to isolate, pick apart the bonds of fellowship, and destroy from the inside out. For the person who listens to gossip, those tasty trifles go down into the inward parts and lead to controversy (Proverbs 18:8).

Most likely, the initial controversy will be based on a small and relatively unimportant matter: A personality conflict. A movement toward an interesting theological stance that doesn't affect anyone's salvation. Perhaps it's somewhat more concerning (e.g., someone has an unwise habit of spending long periods of time with the opposite gender and waives off all well-intentioned warnings with either a laugh or sarcasm). There might be a genuine issue at root, and the recipient of the message is being stubborn and willful in rejecting good counsel.

However, these small controversies (unavoidable in the elbow-jostling that happens in a tightly knit community) will be expanded rather than reduced by the presence and action of a wolf. He will see an opportunity to drive a wedge between believers, a crowbar of sorts. The wedge will grow into a nearly impassible gulf.

In the second step, the gossip train will add a few cars and pick up some speed, like a train rolling downhill. People will get looped in who do not need to be involved at any level. The few who resist will be accused of either not caring about the issue, which now takes on massive implications, or wanting to bury their heads in the sand.

A sign of unhealthy controversy is that frequently after worship, or in each other's homes, congregants will spend quite a bit of time in argument about things that truly are secondary or tertiary in nature. Add the danger of misinterpreting Scripture, and you've got a great way to endlessly discuss the meaning of words or of meaning itself, without coming to a satisfactory conclusion.

A third step is the manufacturing of anger, jealousy, and strife. People get upset because they are not developing the *"unity of the Spirit in the bond of peace"* (Ephesians 4:3).[22] Jealousy happens because some people seem to be superior to others, in works or in words, and competitive streaks surface. Strife happens when family members get into each other's faces, without resolving real differences, and both sides walk away angry until the next bout of verbal sparring. The difference between a family that likes to wrestle (versus a family whose identity lies in fighting) is that no one in the fighting family becomes good friends after the fight. A grudging cessation of active hostility is the only resolution allowed, and no one gets to relax.

---

[22] Note: Unity does not mean that everyone agrees on everything, but it does mean that Christ is the unifying factor and the reason why the congregation exists.

The natural trajectory for group controversy and strife leads to the fourth step: descent into public dissension. One part of the congregation will want to break away because of the endless wrangling that goes unresolved. Sometimes, that breakaway group will announce its intent at an annual meeting. "We've had it. None of you want to listen, and this issue will destroy the church. Goodbye." And the wolf and his followers stick their noses in the air and walk out, leaving a lot of broken, hurting people behind who don't really know what's happened.

Laying a Foundation for a Cult

Now that the wolf pack has formed a group of followers, who believe they have been saved from a horrible congregation, the groundwork can be laid for a cult.

Misapplication of Understanding

> *"They make much of you, but for no good purpose. They want to shut you out, that you may make much of them."*
>
> *—Galatians 4:17*

Like the legalism party in Galatians 4, a cult will offer attractive solutions to vulnerable people, continually promoting practices it will not follow:

- Vulnerability and rest
- Order and justice
- Peace and joy
- Love and understanding.

Our current culture encourages the growth of cults by asserting that if something seems wrong, the whistleblower is probably at fault (because all people intend to do well). The advice given to observers is that instead of making an assessment, the potential whistleblower should dig into a person's background like a trained psychologist to see what makes them tick. This is a terrible way to encourage real transparency or real accountability for human evil because all the emphasis is on "understanding." If only the observer walked a mile in the shoes of the wolf, the negative behavioral patterns would make sense.

With an eye toward domination, wolves use a platform of exclusion to force sheep to "understand" them and their needs. The sheep are made to conform to the wolves' every whim, and any terrified bleat of distress is explained as a lack of understanding on the sheep's part.

Gaining New Followers: Binge-and-Purge Cycles

In a false fold, part of the confusion stems from a massive whirlpool of activity. One month, all focus is on evangelism. Next month, you suddenly don't see a person you always see. You're a little worried to ask questions. Give or take a few years, you hardly notice as people come and go because it happens all the time. The group grows and reduces cyclically. Even when a group expands exponentially, the inner circle remains to make all the real decisions. Since the inner circle isn't affected by ebb and flow, the purging can happen more quietly than in a smaller group.

New people are recruited through some kind of unique "hook." Since the wolf has risen to a respected station in life in the community at large, he can go patrolling for new followers, building customized connections on a continual basis. Perhaps the wolf tells them a sad story about being abandoned, and they, too, feel abandoned. Perhaps the wolf unlocks esoteric mysteries about love, the end times, or prophecy. Perhaps the wolf is well-versed in all things scientific or mathematic. Possibly his followers are skilled at handling questions, and so the follower thinks, "I have found my tribe, my group."

Next will be a proving process, not unlike hazing or a job interview. The new follower has to prove a lack of desire to question authority, or a willingness to learn, to be admitted to the closely guarded group. It's like trying to break into prison instead of out.

The Guilt Cycle

What the follower does not know is that the proving process never ends. Leaders will raise persistent questions about the group's effectiveness or impact, leading to a guilt cycle ("Have I done enough for this group that has done so much for me, giving me new purpose," etc.) with a furious activity cycle to follow, but it is never enough. You can never prove yourself enough to wolves because, despite their arrogance and pride, they are unstable. They never know when another follower will turn on them and express something other than lifelong loyalty. Former betrayers must be vigilant in watching their own backs.

Other followers will observe this endless cycle of proving and will adapt it to their own devices. This web wrapped around the false fold is very strong and seems nearly unbreakable. Even if others beckon from the outside, it's as if they are the shadow people, mouthing words through a dark glass that cannot really be heard.

Followers may prefer to become medicated or experience heavy bouts of depression rather than leave. Where can they go? They have told all their friends and family about this wonderful group, invited them to come to services, or in some way become alienated by their strange devotion. By the time a follower wants to leave, few groups are available to join.

Misapplication of Excommunication

If followers begin to ask questions about the group's purpose or method, it's not unusual for the group to go through some form of purging. This could mean excommunication, or it could mean that the particular psychological warfare practiced by the wolf includes periods of blowing hot and cold. A wolf's zeal does not have a restorative effect.

In a regular church setting, excommunication is the absolute last end of the line because Christians are meant to gain strength in fellowship. Within a wolf's "congregation," excommunication is a tool to be dangled over the head of the fellowship for daring to buck the system or talk back to the leader. There may be some bare minimum of a process in place, more of a box-checker than anything else, but the real intent is to bring people into the following and then make it difficult for them to leave.

It's a mental game of kidnapping. The wolf has access to someone or something that the follower wants. If the follower follows conscience, shows uneasiness, or leaves, she experiences collateral damage. Friends will shun her. In grocery stores, acquaintances will pretend she doesn't exist.

The former follower will feel abandoned, rejected, and isolated. Either the wolf will follow after with encouragement to rejoin after a time of softening or, most likely, just wait for the follower to return with tail between legs. The wolf does not care what happens to the followers after they leave the lair/false fold. The only thing that matters is maintaining a fascinating hold over the rest of the group.

Following the wolf is an all-consuming process. He may intentionally become matchmaker, thus tying followers' marriages inextricably to himself (or a reminder of him). Possibly he will encourage a great deal of activity so the loyal and devoted follower has no time to devote to any other pursuits. The life pattern becomes church activities, family activities, work, and sleep. Hobbies are only useful and recommended if they open opportunities for developing more followers.

Signs of the Endless Cycle: The Cult of Personality

This is an accurate depiction of what happens when a sheep gets sucked into the undertow of a cult or cult-like group inside an existing congregation, led by a manipulator.

Whether the sheep ever really escapes the manipulator depends on the breakaway stage. Physical escape is not the true goal.

Early days

- You're fascinated by the wolf. He looks vital and real and quite different from anyone else.

- The wolf seems to win every argument. In every story he tells about someone else, he never loses. You start to think he's unbeatable.

- Every sermon by the current pastor makes points you've heard before or you think are now irrelevant, while your new leader shows more passion and drive than current leadership.

- You're so glad to be on this person's team. You're starting to think it might be bad if he were your enemy. You dismiss this thought as disloyal.

- You decide to leave with the wolf leader, who says that this congregation is on a path of destruction. Hallelujah, now you're on the right train with the right people!

- You wish that everyone in your former church would have joined the cause and hope that maybe they will join later.

Early warning signs

- The leader does something bad and you don't quite believe the explanation. You have trouble explaining his behavior or repeating his justification(s) for something others see as arrogance or extreme selfishness. Well, everyone is a sinner.

- During times of opposition (i.e., someone has an issue with the leader's behavior or proclamations), you comfort yourself that everyone in the Bible received resistance at first. Paul was not immediately accepted in Acts. Job's three friends badgered him until he was nearly demented. Everything worked out just fine in the end.

- A television show or movie character reminds you of the leader making an excuse. It's safer to get really irritated at the character for the same behavior that you would excuse in the person you know. (Prophet Nathan/King David scenario, II Samuel 12:7.)

In the mud

- You can't read the Bible because it's annoying—or seems like just words on a page. So either you read your favorite parts or you read writings about the Bible that help to hone positions that you're taking.

- Most of your trusted circle (friends and family) show hesitancy or distrust in your current leader, and while you won't admit it, you'd accept their reasoning as valid if you didn't already feel obligated.

- You start to feel trapped and occasionally lash out at friends and family for being unsupportive.

- When you try to explain the leader's brilliance to someone outside the group, it sounds false and echoes in your own ears, so you excuse that disconnect by saying it's somehow that other person's fault for not understanding. It helps if that person is part of a minority group.

- The leader does something bad again. Contrary to common sense and past behavior, you hope that a recent interaction will spark change. If life would just return to normal, you wouldn't have to admit that you were wrong.

- Your prayers are not being answered positively. Everything seems to be going wrong for no apparent reason. The leader claims it's persecution or Satan's harassment, but you just feel continual annoyance, frustration, and dread.

Feeling trapped (emotional roller coaster)

- The more you offer to the leader, the less he provides, giving only more empty promises. You're starting to hate the sight of his face and voice but feel that you can't leave.

- Sometimes you think about walking out of the house or your job and never coming back, without telling anyone.

- You wake up at night in a cold sweat, wondering how you got to this point and how you will get out.

- You increase avoidance techniques when asked to spend time with people outside the leader's group because then you'd have to answer questions. You don't want to talk about what's happened lately, because all your dreams have gone wrong. You wish people would stop being nosy and also wonder why they don't call.

The cause becomes the burden

- The original leader has created an inner circle, and you don't have enough hours in the day to do your work and everything necessary to prop up the leadership team's ever-increasing goals/ideas/dreams. You start thinking about just saying no.

- When you protest that you're tired, either you get a subtle guilt trip about doing the Lord's work or a "gentle encouragement" that maybe you're spending too much time with people outside of the cause; it's your fault for losing focus or becoming burdened with the cares of this world.

- You feel resentful for all of the time spent on the cause that has netted zero real results. People come and go as if your group has a revolving door.

- In dreams, you're drowning or getting into a car accident or trying to talk to people you know—and your mouth is sewn shut. Danger is everywhere. You try to fight and your arms won't move. Your shouts come out in a whisper.

- Everything outside the group or in the future seems dark, uncertain—and frightening. Going out there might be worse than staying.

Time and energy drain

- No one in your group engages in hobbies they used to enjoy. Everyone's time is spoken for, and others are looking just as tired as you.

- You start wondering aloud, with others, what it would be like to control your own calendar. Other followers may bring up historical examples of great leaders (William Carey, William Wilberforce, etc.) who experienced resistance when building the kingdom. They reached their goals in the end.

- One day, you start wondering about ROI—will you ever be paid back for the time and effort you've spent in the group or with its leaders? What has all of this been for? You dismiss this disloyal thought and its implications ("I'm in too deep to back out now"), knowing that you're just afraid to make another mistake.

Conflict (and aftermath)

- Finally, the leadership group does something (or fails to stop someone from doing something awful) that snaps your eyes open. No, you can't take it, and you won't. You gather supporters or enforcers, either to

communicate about breaking ties or confront them
face-to-face.

- The confrontation doesn't go as planned. Either they
  sadly and quietly ask you why you're giving in to
  discouragement when things are going so well (this
  only comes out when you're about to pull support)
  and act righteously angry (how could you do this to
  me who has sacrificed so much), or they flat-out deny
  the accusation or evidence.

- You return home to think things over. It would be
  foolish to make a change in the heat of the moment.
  Perhaps there's a good explanation. Maybe you're just
  prideful or crazy!

- You reevaluate, maybe with friends—or a counselor
  or an attorney. This third party assures you that their
  "explanation" is just deflected criticism or piled-on
  guilt tripping without offering a credible reason for
  their actions. You feel silly but relieved—because
  someone else is seeing what you are seeing.

The breakaway (in stages)

- If the topic begins to circulate in the group, the
  leader(s) continue to deny and evade. Maybe for
  months. You start to hope the leader(s) will die and
  the charade will be over.

- After a few rounds, you realize that their conscience
  has been seared. They will never admit wrong—even
  to themselves. They're not coming back from the pit
  they have dug with their own hands.

- Like a gnawing rodent, your brain can't leave the problem alone. Could you have done something better? Could you have shocked them or forced them to see what they did? You realize you're trying to rescue them again.

- To cope, you write pages in your journals, focus on running, or walk in circles and talk to yourself. Maybe your way of coping is to smoke, obsess verbally with your spouse, or play endless video games, driven to succeed at something. Meanwhile, this problem is eating a hole in your heart and mind.

- The problem is made public. Either someone else found out or the authorities (church or civil) take over. You start to breathe easier. It's obvious the leader(s) habitually ignore every person's advice, not just yours.

Cleanup begins

- The leaders are gone from your life—either they left or you left. You breathe a sigh of relief and start picking up the garbage they left behind. The garbage can is quickly full, and you know there's a long way to go—but the sun has come out from behind the clouds. You start to feel hope.

- You meet someone who reminds you of that person or the group. You get the shakes—in fear or anger. Everything they did comes flooding back. Memories are making you ill. You understand why people rock back and forth, back and forth. It's happening on the inside, like the garbage was never taken out.

Round #2

- A group of new people appears in your congregation—they use the same phrases, or the same voice intonations or implications, or exhibit the same manipulative behavior. You try to convince someone—anyone—of the danger. Your new friends haven't been through the process, so they don't quite believe you. Surely there's a good explanation! You feel panic at their ignorance; it will drag you into the undertow.

- You dig up a lot of old history to convince the skeptic that it's the same situation, different face. The skeptic remains skeptical. Why would such nice people do the exact same thing as that person in your apocryphal stories? The chances of that happening twice are like being struck twice by lightning; you must be paranoid. These people just want to do good things, and they're sincere brothers/sisters in Christ. Sure, they're a little too focused, but they'll calm down with time. You shake your head because egotists don't calm down.

- For the good of everyone, to preserve unity, you tell yourself, "I will attempt to get along and make friends" despite the wobbly feeling in your stomach. The skeptic wants you to put those ghosts of the past to rest and believe that things can be different. Perhaps it's just perception and paranoia—you just don't want to be healed.

Following #2

- You start planning for the future. "I will not say 'I told you so' when they show their true faces.'" You can't relax in their presence; you are always on guard, and maybe even record conversations. You know others consider that you have let old history color the present reality, but you can't do much about those perceptions. You have lived through something they have not experienced, and don't want to experience.

- The new group finally does something visible—a power grab, an attempt at division, or a sketchy excuse. Perhaps the skeptic even begins to think they might have issues. But no one wants to address those issues because the new group is very influential—and aggressive.

- You feel angry and sad and let down all at the same time. You were not protected, no one believed you, and now there will be trouble that you wanted to avoid. No one listened, and you feel resentful.

Breakaway #2

- Either you go to the authorities (church or civil) and try to make your points again about the obvious failure, you try to make friends with the skeptics who see what you've been saying all along, or the skeptics stubbornly maintain that you're just blinded by prejudice.

- The church wreckers move on, preying on vulnerable people on the edge of the Christian life: loners, dissatisfied, desperate people looking for a home.

- Meanwhile, your church group avoids responsibility in spreading the word that these are bad people with bad intentions, who look believable while telling lies and never, ever take responsibility. It's all someone else's fault.

After having taken the immediate first steps, you have a few choices for your next steps.

Your Reaction	The Reality
You get bitter about the injustice and you talk about it for the rest of your life. At least you're not silent.	It's never really resolved and you may never truly heal.
You keep silent and decide to live a life of peace. No one needs to hear your story, right?	It's never really resolved and you may never truly heal.
You take on the wolf with others, and they get subdued for a while.	You realistically assume that either the wolves will try again, or there will be other wolves.
You mend ties with the people who were genuinely deceived, in slow and steady increments of trust-building.	You realize that just because they also got trapped with the wolf doesn't necessarily mean they are wolves.

Your Reaction	**The Reality**
You move to another area and resolve to never repeat the cycle. You know the warning signs now.	Either you find another wolf or you realize that you didn't quite address something the last time. You resolve to address it now.
You decide that the whole problem is with the institutionalized church. They're all hypocrites. You and Jesus are the only necessary moral majority.	Welcome to the hypocrite club. You're a founding member and may turn into a wolf, especially on social media.

It is wretchedly frustrating to have to obey protocol when wolves adhere to no one's orders but their own. So it can be tempting to bend rules or dispense with them altogether—go vigilante. But when sheep get the idea that the Shepherd is unable or unwilling to engage in defense or protection, they paint targets on their own backs for a destroyer far cleverer than themselves.

Remember, your true enemy is also the ultimate pragmatist. Satan does not care about the means of destruction, only the result. He is just as wickedly happy with God's people being maimed by a wolf (external destruction) or eaten alive by unresolved bitterness (internal destruction). He will turn the desire for good into evil, and count it as a success.

Hang on to the fact that God will bring to light every deed done in secret (Luke 8:17). The fact that there is an actual Hell—not a theoretical one—makes sense when one realizes that leopards don't change their spots, wolves don't change their nature, and Satan will experience eternal punishment.

Is it a Cult or Just Sin?

This is a tricky question. Many Christian splinter groups like to label some other group as a cult or say that orthodoxy is dead. This becomes an excuse for many wolves to either engage in competitive and ever-stricter neo-orthodoxy or dream up outlandish worship practices (like barking in the Spirit) that set any normal Christian's teeth on edge and their hair on fire.

A true cult will have these characteristics:

- Formulas—Wolves use formulas to pounce on the person who is out of compliance, blaming their every distress on the "rebel" being out of step with the formula. Every cult indicates by word and deed that sheep must be controlled (not just directed or organized) by a human force. Jesus, His Word, and His teachings aren't enough to keep them in line.

- On the fringe—Whether a Unitarian, a mystic, or an uber-theological type, the wolf ascribes to some outlandish understanding claiming the Bible as its true foundation. Everyone from 100 AD onward has been wrong about X topic. To *really* understand the Bible, you have to move away from Y doctrine, commonly understood for many centuries, in favor of Z author who really puts things into perspective. Everything is going wrong for the church because of this belief (x). Everything will change in the church if we all take a steady diet of (z), whose devotees act like angry monks in a cloister, engage in group shouting at sinners on street corners, or some other on-the-fringe, cringeworthy habit.

- Going deeper—False teachers have a manic drive to go beyond normal Biblical topics, diving deeper into really strange areas lightly covered in very few passages of Scripture. They may develop code words to encapsulate the greatness of these topics.

- Beauty and truth—Some wolves, just to be different, gaze with soulful and "hurt" eyes when you try to make them define exactly what they mean. They go on for paragraphs about the soul and its true ability to frolic in nature, and how everything material is not quite top-drawer. In reality, these are the worst materialists on the planet. They love money. Mystic theology is a great way to pull the wool over people's eyes, getting drunk with words at the expense of anything definite.

It is possible for a former cult member to become an orthodox member of the faith and even a bona fide leader. Augustine of Hippo dabbled in a few on-the-fringe movements before the light dawned, but his legacy has lasted for centuries.

A DAMAGED CONGREGATION

After a wolf has infiltrated a congregation and taken some of the flock, the congregation is left to deal with the damage. It may help to know that nothing short of a God-ordained spiritual heart transplant could effect any change.

Picking up the Pieces

In the aftermath of this spiritual hurricane, unresolved questions can lead to a lack of peace in the congregation and then to a feeling of hopelessness.

- What went wrong?
- How can we be right again?
- If we had prayed harder, with more faith, would God have changed hearts?
- If we had acted differently, would there have been a better result?

Sometimes outside observers will offer truisms in an effort to be helpful, and it drives the feeling of failure deeper. Prayer is powerful and moves mountains, but the time to mention that is not after a congregation has survived a takeover attempt. Also, phrases about miraculous changes or blanket forgiveness should not be applied as a panacea, any more than one should say, "Time heals all wounds" at a funeral or a divorce hearing.

Further, a few passages in the Word (including Hebrews 10) indicate that there is no point in praying for someone who is determined to remain in their sins.

There is truly no point in praying after they are dead (Deuteronomy 18:11), as those wolves who counted themselves as part of the fellowship will be utterly rejected by Jesus on that last day. *"Depart from me"* (Matthew 7:23). He never knew them, so their works and their words about Him are utterly worthless.

Nor is it helpful to offer bromides about prevention being worth more than a pound of cure, as though it's helpful to point fingers at the congregation after the fence has fallen down. Prevention only goes so far, and wolves infiltrating a congregation is inevitable. No congregation can prevent sin from happening, because it lives in the human heart and inclinations. Believers can only do a few things: see warning signs, interpret them effectively (with the aid of the Spirit), use discernment, and try to mitigate damage. No one person or group can stop the suffering and refining process because this is a major part of God's work in His people.

The drama and bad feelings take a while to get over. The congregation has experienced a hostile force bent on taking over, and it takes some intentional redirection to move past that experience. Learning to "weep with those who weep" is better than being an armchair theologian.

Moving through Reactions

Congregations who effectively deal with predators while continuing to live in peaceful submission to God are as rare and blessed as the Israelites in Joshua's time. They obeyed God's Word, they settled the rebellious land around them, and they were willing to contend with straying parts of the tribes of Israel.

More than likely, wolf-bitten congregations will experience one or all the unhelpful reactions discussed below. The important part is to not turn them into a lifelong habit:

- Drama kings/queens—They incorporate drama into their lives; it becomes a cyclical habit of rejection and inclusion into the home and heart. Anything attention-grabbing will be a focal point of conversation: the good, the bad, and the ugly.

- Paranoia—They fear any return to that particular time in the past and do everything in their power to stop a recurrence.

- Panic—They feel heart-pounding anxiety in the presence of anyone who reminds them of that time.

- Avoidance—They want to move on quickly, as though it never happened, in the hopes that time will bring healing so they just "get on with life."

At some point, the congregation must intentionally move on, but they must first actively heal. It certainly helps if the wolves do not return. If wolves return repeatedly, this may be a sign that the congregation is either suffering from the first reaction of drama addiction or has an allergic reaction to becoming healed because they don't know how to operate in a healthy way.

Whether the group has become anemic, lukewarm, or has contracted some form of group blindness (or Alzheimer's), *it has something that the wolf wants.* There is some specific reason for the congregation to engage with the same type of predators without resolution.

ACTION:
A CONGREGATION'S
RESPONSIBILITY

"If your brother sins against you, go and tell him his fault, between you and him alone. If he listens to you, you have gained your brother. [16] *But if he does not listen, take one or two others along with you, that every charge may be established by the evidence of two or three witnesses.* [17] *If he refuses to listen to them, tell it to the church. And if he refuses to listen even to the church, let him be to you as a Gentile and a tax collector.* [18] *Truly, I say to you, whatever you bind on earth shall be bound in heaven, and whatever you loose on earth shall be loosed in heaven.* [19] *Again I say to you, if two of you agree on earth about anything they ask, it will be done for them by my Father in heaven.* [20] *For where two or three are gathered in my name, there am I among them."*

—Matthew 18:15–20

Pray actively. Pray unceasingly. Since you're dealing with a deep level of deception, it's good to have Jesus's mentality about the removal of particular evil spirits, which *"never comes out except by prayer and fasting"* (Matthew 17:21). Wolves actively engage in spiritual war, and prayer is one of your primary defenses.

Read the Scriptures. Gaining familiarity with the Word helps in predicting the wolves' next moves because Satan is not creative. He has endless variations on the same themes: rebellion, dissension, anger, malice, gossip, slander, and eventually murder. Reading through Acts, James, and I and II Peter is helpful in spotting the trends and making connections.

Stand by your (good) leaders. The leaders of any church should be taking the lead in handling wolves. If they are addressing problems with problem people, let them do it with support and without interference. However, wolves can sometimes float under the radar or fool the leaders, and the elders cannot be everywhere at once.

If the leaders in your church avoid dealing with conflict, this makes interaction harder. The wolf will sense weakness and be quite willing to exploit the chinks in the leaders' armor. Wolves will tackle the weakest links, but God does say that He delights in using the weak to *"shame the strong"* (I Corinthians 1:27).

Matthew 18: Golden Rule of Conflict Resolution

In addition to a real and heartfelt number of hours on their knees, congregants can do four things based on Matthew 18:

Tackle the issue with the problem person. This first point cannot be overemphasized, because (1) most people who notice something do not take direct action, and (2) Matthew 18 clearly outlines direct action as the first step in the process. Speak personally and individually with the person causing the issue, then follow up with action points. While it's helpful to leave a private corner of your mind open to the possibility of being in the wrong, any verbal assertion of hesitancy or accommodation to a wolf paints a large target on your back and indicates that you are prey. In essence, dealing with wolves means that you cannot be vulnerable with them, as you would be with a trusted friend. If the issue is real and not just a personal preference, it needs to be dealt with clearly and not in the shadows.

When you tackle the issue, challenge them with the Word. In Matthew 4, Jesus showed a consistent way to defeat Satan. The Word, the sword of the Lord, is our weapon that does not change. If you can, show how the reinterpretation of Scripture is wrong. The idea of pointing out someone else's error makes many kind, humble people very nervous, but it is not possible to ignore a wolf out of existence.

The main point of this meeting is not to "win" the argument but for true colors to be shown. If the wolf is not merely a headstrong sheep that has forgotten humility, it will become apparent that he (or she) has no interest in change—only in blame.

Use strength in numbers. After an initial meeting establishing the issue and the boundaries, do not allow yourself to be brought over "for a private discussion to work things out" or be taken hostage over the phone. The wolf's problem is not your problem. Endless rounds of either (a) engaging in emotional manipulation ("someone just needs to hear about how this has affected me") or (b) attacks on your faith ("you're not much of a believer since you did *X*") can be a sign that your estimation of this person's character was on point. Going two-by-two to tackle difficult topics, either in witnessing the good news or in witnessing a person's real resistance to resolving conflict, holds a great deal of spiritual and legal sense.

You could have multiple group follow-up meetings around wolves until they have been neutralized or made ineffective. While just one group meeting may not be enough, the plain reading of the Matthew 18 passage seems to indicate a few instances before leading to a resolution.

The reason to catch a wolf in a lie is not so that the wolf actually changes, but so the sheep can be shown they have been duped by the wolf's act.

Speak with leaders about the issue and press for action. While showing a respectful attitude to authority, if the leader fails to understand the nature of the problem, bring along witnesses— other sheep who have experienced something of the wolves' inevitable gossip, dissension, or wrangling of words. Make a good case of it, and do not back down unless they prove your impressions are really wrong. Real sin cannot be left in a closet or under the bed even if you are the one who is wrong and needs to repent.

If the leaders are squeamish about bringing truth to light because of eventual consequences or hurt feelings and if it is a Biblical issue that warrants discipline, the leaders must be challenged to apply Scripture where people live. It is a living, active Word, not a dead letter.

But note that you are to press for action, not go digging yourself. Even stated leaders' foot-dragging does not authorize an individual as "the called one" to uncover evidence or go digging like an unholy treasure hunter, an investigator gone wrong. God will reveal that evidence at the proper time. If you have a piece of that evidence already, it should be sent to the proper authorities. If no one has given you the job of digging, sometimes it is best to leave well enough alone.

Ask Questions. If the wolf calls for multiple invitations for a private meeting to "clarify," this can be an opportunity to bring along a church leader (especially a reluctant one). Start the meeting by asking questions. "Why did we need to meet? Why did you insist on this being a private meeting?" Haul out into the light the thing that the wolf most wants to keep secret. He may pretend to be hurt, and you may be the subject of some vicious gossip for a while. Remember the main way that sheep are allowed a defense is to stand firm. If the Ephesians 6 armor fits, you cannot be touched—those fiery darts might sting, and some may need to be plucked out. Just don't let them get to the heart.

While an accommodating spirit is great for dealing with true brothers and sisters in Christ, it is good to resist the devil so that he flees. Once the wolf has been clearly identified, refuse to dance to his tune. When dealing with a spiritually schizophrenic person, a trail of evidence should lead to some sort of real consequence.

Remove the Wolf from the Flock

You may wonder how the admonition to "take it to the church" from Matthew 18 can be applied without engaging a lot of people in gossip.

One great explanation is that the church members who have the ability of final resolution are the elders. When they meet together to decide something, they have the ability to make final determinations—like a court, with Jesus as the Judge.

If you can, find an under-shepherd with a heavy staff who isn't afraid to pin down the wolf. He only ever understands a show of strength. The wolf will then run off and howl, to whatever flock or moon is available, about how he was so ill-treated, so damaged, and his trust so abused. Soon the wolf will begin with another flock and attempt to recreate the cycle; if you remember that the wolf's problem is rejection of authority rather than unmet needs,[23] that will prevent you from feeling responsibility for his choices.

---

[23] Abraham Maslow created the theory of a multi-level pyramid, the hierarchy of needs; the latest version showed self-transcendence at the pinnacle.

So to effectively remove the wolf, expose him (or her) to the proper authority; whether this happens once or multiple times depends on the situation and your desired level of involvement. As a result, you will find yourself caught up in some spiritual warfare. If you stay the course and refuse to concede power, this will be to your benefit long term. Developing a reputation for openly dealing with issues has a dual benefit: it will make a wolf more wary of tangling with you while also making you a stronger follower of Christ.

Exposure: Caught in the Lie

The first thing is to expose them, as this is one of the things that wolves most fear. They will become furious if you penetrate their disguise and strings of lies. They will seek to discredit you in every way possible. They will fight, they will tear, they will use every guilt-inducing, heart-wrenching method to keep their true nature from being brought into the light. Be aware that no words from them about peace means it lives in their hearts.

For example, if the issue is well-known, you might organize an open forum to haul out all the whispered issues in public. This has the best chance of success with church or civil authorities who show evidence of buy-in. If the leaders balk at openness, it's a great time to ask why action isn't being taken or set deadlines with expectations. If the issue has gathered media attention, be aware that the open forum may be your last meeting with the group.

If there are meetings with elders in a closed forum, the ground rules of interaction must be followed consistently. Resist last-minute changes on the basis of lack of time since every change is more likely to benefit wolves than sheep. (Predators maneuver easily.)

Remember that any individual makes an easier target than a pair or a group. When possible, avoid being cut out of the sheepfold. If information is requested, provide it at the time and place of your choosing. If a third party's cooperation is requested, require that this person's actual personal views and wishes be respected so "cooperation" is not allowed to turn into coercion.

If a closed church meeting is demanded as necessary, keep wolves from gaining the upper hand. It can be delayed beyond the "necessary" (aka immediate) timeframe. You can tell the individuals up front that it will be recorded, or you will refuse to attend. State clearly why a closed meeting is completely unnecessary, a la Nehemiah telling enemies that they were imagining baseless charges and he was far too busy to waste time with them (Nehemiah 6:8). There is no reason for a sheep to be backed into a corner and then told what to do by someone other than a bona fide shepherd.

As soon as they are exposed, watch out. Snarling. Ravening. Denial. Accusation. Attempts to discredit. Crying about meanness, arrogance, and deceit. You'll get the works. And if you try to describe it later, it sounds. . . . demented.

Spiritual Warfare: Not a Gentleman's Game

Once wolves are exposed, expect to be caught up in some confusing rounds of spiritual warfare that will not adhere to any sort of Geneva Convention. Wolves often get their way because Christians are far too malleable in agreeing to do whatever the squeaky wheel wants to be done, or because Christians expect their enemies to behave with decency and decorum. Appeasement of a wolf is a one-way road to disappointment and failure. Apply the same tactics to the follower of Satan as to Satan: the Word, prayer, and resistance to evil. Especially resist the urge toward revenge.

Just be aware that even if you do right by following the Matthew 18 process, it's likely your in-person interview won't go well. The wolf may take an offensive tactical approach by throwing a calculated guilt trip or storming out after making you feel in the wrong. Afterward, you may wonder, "Didn't I have the right to say no?" In the wolf's mind, no one has a valid second option. You never have the right to do anything other than what the wolf wants.

If the wolf takes an indirect tactical approach by gossiping to sheep fooled by the disguise, you may need to repeat your decision against niceness to another kindly soul who will ask in concern, "Why didn't you help Brother *X* or Sister *Y*?" Perhaps your integrity will be called into question. Possibly you'll have to answer to a higher authority, either on trumped-up charges or because there's some sneaky rumor that you're holding on too tightly to an aspect of church life.

Refuse to Agree or Concede Power

If they start this spiritual warfare, refuse to fight on their terms, on their turf, or with their definitions. Wolves develop their own vocabulary and often insist (subtly or directly) that you use their words to defeat them. That's like David going out into battle using Saul's armor (I Samuel 17:39). If you try to use armor that you haven't tested, going out against a larger and more experienced warrior, you will fumble with tools made for someone else. Just use the tools that you have, with which you're already comfortable.

You don't have to agree with their individual definition of the Holy Spirit's work, healings, miracles, or church growth. You don't have to agree with their version of Jesus as anyone other than the historical Person described in the Bible. You don't have to agree with their method of evangelism, just because they happen to like it.

Personal anecdotes about the effectiveness of the idea are often immaterial because they do not point back to the truth. The Word is like your anchor; it will keep the vessel from being dashed to pieces when its captain is being tossed to and fro by opinions of man. God forbid that you become a shipwrecked soul, simply out of fear of another sailor's opinion.

Pattern Disruption: A Key to Success

The real way to destroy the wolves' intentions is to disrupt their usual successful pattern. Think about what they usually do that produces anger, strife, and bad feelings over the long term. Move in the opposite direction.

Wolves flee from the light of scrutiny, they hate being told what to do, and both of those things are absolutely necessary to keep the flock from harm. Allowing a lack of discipline to rebels under the guise of kindness does not help. Sometimes, insisting on the presence of police officers can have a chilling effect on manipulative efforts. Wolves tend to act less predatory when sheepdogs are around.

Work scenario: Pattern disruption (external)[24]

> *"Failure to plan is a plan to fail."*
> —Old leadership phrase

Let's say that a well-known, highly connected leader in a Christian organization has a habit of walking into women's offices and bringing up his unhappy marriage. Once or twice, he cozies up to a female, who is wondering how to end the uncomfortable conversation, and places his hand on her knee. What is she to do in this scenario?

While the female has more than a few options, it is completely understandable that (in most cases) those options are rarely enacted. The usual prey responses are much more common. (In this case, victims often experience the body betrayal freeze response so common to prey: "I can't believe this is happening. When will it stop?")

Single parents are especially vulnerable in the workplace, because they are usually breadwinners. Idealists are even more vulnerable because they just do not understand how this could happen in such a good organization. It is a wretched shame that wolves seek every opportunity to exploit vulnerability.

---

[24] "The greatest evil is not now done in those sordid 'dens of crime' that Dickens loved to paint. It is not done even in concentration camps and labour camps. In those we see its final result. But it is conceived and ordered (moved, seconded, carried, and minuted) in clean, carpeted, warmed, and well-lighted offices, by quiet men with white collars and cut fingernails and smooth-shaven cheeks who do not need to raise their voice. Hence, naturally enough, my symbol for Hell is something like the bureaucracy of a police state or the offices of a thoroughly nasty business concern." C.S. Lewis, preface to *Screwtape Letters*, page xxv.

If something like this happens one time, she might be able to chalk it up to the difficulties of life. If it happens a second time—she needs a plan. The active-shooter protocol suggests three options (run, hide, or fight), but applied in this office setting, the running option usually just means handing in your notice. Let's consider the more complex options based on fighting or hiding.

Option 1 Fight (Snow Queen): Glare coldly at the knee-grabber and inform him that either he removes himself from your office or he will be eating a paperweight, followed up with a report to HR. Possibly a call to his wife.

Hide (Support Group): Randomly overhear another victim complaining about the leader getting too cozy and experience a rush of "so it wasn't just me" feelings, then perhaps invite the other victim into conversation. Both victims feel comforted but still violated.

Option 2 Fight (Investigate): Include the other victim in a meeting with an attorney and discuss the next steps. Possibly reach out to the police and find out if the knee-grabbing leader has any past history related to your incident.

Hide (Freeze): Experience the "freeze" response, heave a sigh of relief when an interruption occurs, and do everything possible to ensure you open-door policy means the physical door stays open. Team up with other victims to guardedly warn new recruits about the leader's habits and suggest scarves or high-necked sweaters as a solution to being ogled in meetings.

Option 3 Fight (Execute a plan): Submit a report to HR, and inform them that if they choose the cover-up or do-nothing response, your next step will be to inform a member of the civil authorities and then the press. (It helps if you already have a name and an email address to use.)

Hide (Avoid): Look for another job and heave a sigh of relief on your last day. The past is behind you; there's no point in digging it up.

Option 4 Fight (Exit Interview): Tell both your supervisor and HR that this organization will need to learn how to deal with sexual harassment like any other. If disciplinary issues are mentioned, it might be handy to have the name and email address of an EEOC investigator. Being eased out via corporate retaliation for whistle-blowing is a serious issue.

Hide (Exit Interview): Gently hint to the interviewer that some training about sexual harassment might be a good idea because you heard some disturbing talk and rumors about people not being treated well. Avoid saying any names or providing any details, because you just want to escape to the other side of the door.

Although this scenario is based in a workplace setting, the leader is a wolf (i.e. predator). The same predatory tactics are at play and the woman (i.e. the object of unwelcome attention) can either be victimized, making "victim" a part of her identity, or take action.

Pattern disruption—Deny yourself victim status (internal)

Jesus offered one of the greatest insights into healing that we've ever heard when he asked the invalid of 38 years, *"Do you want to be healed?"* (John 5:5-6). Do you want to leave this sick community whose issues you know, inside and out? Do you want to become responsible for your own health and welfare and stop depending on others, feeling sad that others aren't helping you? Do you want to get up and walk in the light of truth?

To avoid being exploited, it is important to find out how to avoid transmitting signals of visible distress. (Note: Looking like prey is a very natural response). A set of hunched shoulders and a "please, don't hit me" expression does not trigger protective instincts in predators. They see dinner. To avoid becoming dinner, it's important to develop strategic and well-planned responses that replace your natural, fear responses, and it will take effort.

The flip side is also true: going on continual search-and-rescue missions for the misunderstood often ends badly. The underlying pride of the savior complex—masked by the idea that everyone can change—is that one loving individual can essentially have more influence than God chooses to have. He does not intend to bring everyone into Heaven. He does not intend to bring wolves into His eternal fold. They are a temporary earthly tool, and they have an end date.

If you are drawn toward broken souls who seem on the brink of always needing just a little more help, it's possible that the power of Christ is not in the interaction. If so, the best thing would be for that person to fall into real trouble and receive real consequences. If a person doesn't see that they are broken (or want to be fixed), it will be much harder for he or she to accept the help that is required by healing.

Above all, refuse to be distracted by a wolf's never-ending issues. Those issues will never be solved, because wolves do not wish to be healed. They have no intention of loving or obeying God, and nothing that man can do will change them.

Fight Despair and Oppression

> *"How long before You will judge and avenge our*
> *blood on those who dwell on the earth?"*
> *—Revelation 6:10*

When it comes to the feelings of despair and oppression, remember that these (and other) feelings can change. While never welcome, they can be helpful early warning indicators of battle with the enemy, or that something is terribly wrong in the camp. Martin Lloyd-Jones wrote a very good book on *Spiritual Depression,* especially for seasoned believers who have a vague guilty feeling about discouragement, as though their time in spiritual disciplines (the Word, prayer, worship, etc.) should be enough to combat the world, the flesh, and the Devil. The guilt feelings might get crystallized into self-accusations of a failure to progress, in thoughts like these: "Shouldn't I be beyond this point?"

A rather small percentage of the world is fighting hosts of darkness and spiritual forces of evil that are everywhere present. You need others to help you fight despair, which grows in isolation and adds a misery contingent to the cry of the believers under the altar (Revelation 6:10) that echoes the cry of many psalmists: When will there be resolution? In Psalm 13, there is another thought that sometimes appears: Why are You so very angry with us? Sometimes the lack of visible action feels like punishment.

What Is Despair

> *"Be strong and courageous."*
> *—Joshua to the Israelites*

If the wolf can't gain his object (destruction) by a frontal attack, he'll try a sideways attack that gnaws at your vitals and refuses to leave you alone late at night: despair.

Despair is like the hopeless cousin of depression. It works internally, hangs around your neck like a noose, and usually repeats depressing phrases: "It's hopeless. The wolves will just come back again. There doesn't seem to be a point in fighting them. They will never stop."

Also, despair can be sneaky. Sometimes it comes cloaked in discouragement, at other times it swaggers up to you with a devil-may-care smile, flings a red cape around your shoulders, and says winningly, "You only live once." That kind of voice says it's a brave and daring enterprise to jump off a bridge. Once you're nearly in the water, you know it's a problem—but how to get out? The water is deep. Often the rescue boat is either delayed or belongs to an 'altruistic' street pharmaceuticals representative. Help is worthwhile only if it pushes you toward God, not away from Him.

What Is Oppression

> "Do not be surprised at the fiery trial when it comes upon you to
> test you, as though something strange were happening to you".
> Peter to the scattered Jewish believers.
>
> —I Peter 4:12

Oppression is a force outside of yourself or your congregation. When oppression becomes a cloud hanging over the group, it indicates that spiritual strongholds and forces of darkness have taken over, intent on complete destruction of anything good. It may be encouraging to know that you haven't been singled out for anything unusual in the kingdom of God. Peter is very clear that Satan, in general, has it out for all God's children.

How to Fight

"Shall we receive good from God, and shall we not receive evil [adversity]?
—Job 2:10

You may feel suffocated or squashed by the twin forces of despair and oppression because one comes from the inside and one from the outside. How can you fight in this condition? Knowledge and education are of some value, but no one can defeat these forces by brainpower or willpower alone. You fight with God as your captain. God is the tower to whom you run, and under His wings, you are safe. Your own brain is less than helpful when confronting a being of nearly infinite malice who is bent on turning to ashes everything and everyone who offers reminders of God.

The constancy and repetition of the attacks may also be wearing. You fight by standing firm in God's Word. Maybe the wolves keep sending you endless meeting requests, piles of emails, or 50 social media posts per day. Again, they want an "opportunity to clarify" the issues that just won't get resolved. Again, there's an annoying phone call, and you had to hang up on someone who just won't let the hatchet be buried or put down the axe. You're so frustrated that you think about just running away. "What is the point in standing firm?" whispers an old, seemingly friendly voice. It is not a still or quiet voice because it repeats this message at various intervals until you give it the smackdown: the Word. Because God says to stand firm.

You may get a variant of another message: "How can you trust what God says?" You fight in knowing that God is truth. You know quite well that this is not the voice of the Holy Spirit, so there is no point in entertaining it. You cannot defeat it with logic, because faulty logic can look really close to the real thing. You cannot defeat it by distraction, because it will just come back.

It can only be defeated or pushed out by clinging to the truth of the Word.

Really, love is a powerful tool because it is selfless. Love engages in everything the enemy thinks is worthless: hope, faith, perseverance, the long game. Many people have said that the Word is God's love letter to His people. With it, He has handed you the tools that you need to defeat His enemies and yours.

Reminding Ourselves of God's Attributes

> *"And without faith it is impossible to please Him, for whoever would draw near to God must believe that He exists and that He rewards those who seek Him."*
>
> —Hebrews 11:6

While pointing out some things about our enemy, it's necessary to be reminded of God's character to stay grounded.

First, you must recognize that God **is** as well as the Rewarder. No one else occupies the position of both Creator and Savior. No one else has the right to usurp a Creator or Savior role. We can reflect, we can resemble, but we are created beings and nothing close to who He is.

Recognize that God is **sovereign**. As the reigning King of the Universe, He has every right to order His creation to do His will. This means He can do absolutely everything in the way that *He* sees fit, without our input or interference, including the issuance of trials and afflictions. Because His character is of love and kindness and generosity, He voluntarily brings former enemies into His family. His good character is the only thing that stands between us and doom. Any voice that tries to convince you that He is not reliable or trustworthy is automatically a false voice.

Recognize that God is **Father**. He means these trials and afflictions for your good, as well as all of the blessings and common measurements of grace allotted to you. He will do good to those who love Him, *"those who are called according to His purpose"* (Romans 8:28). As a good Father, He is not an overbearing overseer, like some who try to overtake His position.

When you pour out your hurt, frustration, anxiety, and questions to Him, He will not only listen, He will act. Either you will be reminded of His character or the circumstance will change. Love is a very active word. (I listened to the band *DC Talk* at a formative age.)

When Psalmists describe the interaction between man and God, many heartrending issues get resolved by the end of the work. Sometimes the resolution comes out of reminders of a great deal of trust in God as the protector and defender of the helpless (strong tower, eagle's wings, burning fire, etc.). Whether through application of history or assurances that He will finally triumph over enemies, the Psalms are very comforting. God will do what is just, what is right, and what is necessary.

Recognize that God is not **to blame**. While it's popular in some circles to say that you can say anything to God without consequence—that is not what He said to Job. You cannot shake your fist as though He is responsible for man or Satan's devices. He has not authorized evil, nor does He delight in it. In many ways, He has already defeated evil by the destruction of death; we are merely waiting for the final curtain to descend. He limits the effects of evil, although He has destined some of the wicked to do some of His will, as well as for Judgment Day.

Recognize that God is the **judge**. This is stated frequently in the Psalms: God is the avenger of the poor, widow, orphan, and oppressed. He has the right to issue rewards and punishments on that final Day, as mentioned in most of the books of the Bible.

While heavenly joys do await believers, it's also comforting to know that the final book of Revelation could be summed up in this way: Jesus wins. It should comfort us to know that He will do much better with His sword than any earthly, fallible judge—and that bad judges will be called to account for their apathy, partiality, and stupidity.

Reminding Ourselves of Proper Conduct in Prayer

While we have been given powerful weapons of defense (the Spirit, the Word, and prayer), the weight of opposition will still sometimes overwhelm like a tidal wave. At those times, prayer is really your best outlet—crying out to God.

Without being trite, the ACTS acronym is helpful. Prayer should involve a mixture of **A**doration, **C**onfession, **T**hanksgiving, and **S**upplication. However, in Jesus's parable, he did not indicate that the tax collector was wrong for beating his breast only making a single supplication: *"God, be merciful to me, a sinner!"* Sometimes you have to get right to the good stuff.

For an indwelling sin or destruction issue, a little shaking of the gates of Heaven may be required. (This does not mean that you will get an immediate yes; that would make you a victorious bully and not a supplicant. God does not respond positively to spiritual thuggery.)

In I Samuel 1, we are not told whether Hannah mixed her passionate, silent requests for a son with a lot of adoration or confession. (We know the prayer was not answered positively just because Eli was such a great priest.) We do know that God heard her request and was pleased to grant it.

Patience is key. The Lord was also pleased to promise a son to Abraham and Sarah, yet it took 25 years for Isaac to appear.

Use Your Defensive Tools

In my twenties, I became fascinated with castles—their many layers of defense, their strategic locations, and the importance of topography. The surrounding area, on which the castle was built, was just as important as the need for moats, mortar, and strong architecture. At any moment, castle life could move from a humdrum existence to a beehive of activity, either to receive guests or repel invaders. It's not a bad illustration of communal Christian life, as we are called to be watchful (Ezekiel 33, I Corinthians 16:13, etc.).

Guarding your castle involves at least six steps (there may be more):

1. **Run away from danger and toward protection.** This is really a sheep's best defense mechanism: run away from danger, toward the Shepherd. In a very broad sense, Joseph left all to follow Christ when fleeing from temptation (Genesis 39). While Potiphar's wife used this to her advantage, it just underlined her wickedness and his righteousness. As a mark of God's grace, Potiphar did not have Joseph killed. As the military saying goes, "He who fights and runs away, lives to fight another day."

2. **Huddle with other sheep.** If you're just farming on your own, all is well until enemies appear over the horizon. Tough individualism can work with peers, but even angels don't individually stand against the Prince of the Power of the Air (Daniel 10:13). Running away from one major danger just makes you an easy target in the bushes. There's a reason why the parables involving

sheep often involve them individually straggling off to be snared or caught or hurt. Even though some harm can come from huddling with others, it's still better than not knowing when the attacks will come and from which angle. Others are able to see issues that you may overlook and vice versa. That's why the church is referred to as a "body."

3. **Maintain the protective place**. A castle is only as effective against predators on the outside as it is well-provisioned and well-maintained on the inside. Examine any gaps in the walls, transition points choked with weeds (e.g. the moat), and leaders looking sloppy. If the leaders let their armor go unpolished or their swords unsharpened, they need a wake-up call— to arms and to discipline. (Think of Caspian being "welcomed" into Gumpas's region of The Lone Isles in *Prince Caspian*). If you make it inside just to find out that no one set aside stores of grain and potatoes, or that the ovens have fallen into disrepair, you will starve within a matter of weeks. If the water supply is down to a few barrels, you will die within days. Medieval watchmen who fell asleep at their posts were executed because neglect placed everyone in danger. Modern military members can still be court-martialed for this sloppiness.

4. **Strap on armor.** Ephesians 6 uses the illustration of the armor of God as an indication that we are to be warrior sheep. (What a concept!) There's a sword, a shield, footwear, and a helmet. These are all defensive mechanisms. As the Romans found out, you can defeat a powerful enemy by locking shields and moving forward as one unit.

5. **Avoid wasting energy on suicide missions.** Let the enemy come to you, and let them waste a lot of resources hammering at well-barricaded, well-defended doors. Novel insights should be explained from a mixture of Scripture and church history, which has weeded out many pretenders. (Don't be afraid to pour on the boiling oil if they are pounding on your door, demanding to be let in.) It's a dangerous habit to always hunt for the new and esoteric. Knowledge puffs up. Love edifies.

6. **Send missiles from a defended area of safety.** Medieval fighters used a combination of the huddle— inside well-defended layers of walls around castles— and tactical offense methods. Castle defenders brought out their swords after the enemy depleted their energy swarming up a hill, slopping through the flood of garbage thrown into the moats, being shot at from the outer walls, with boiling oil poured on invading forces for good measure. Once the enemy made it through all these outer layers of defense, the game to gain the inner keep began. The enemy may have reached inside the first layer of the wall, but more boiling oil, arrows, and muck were reserved for the second wall before the survivors stormed the keep. If these measures did not deter the enemy, explosives were employed that tore holes in walls, along with some dirty psychological warfare (involving trebuchets with human heads flung over the walls). Sustained attack invited knights on chargers, flaming pitch balls, or a loosed flood of debris to wash the invaders down the hill. If the invaders advanced through all of these layered defenses and reached the inner keep, or heart of the castle (including a well, food storage, and living quarters), the battle was over.

Beware the Lure of Neutrality

In any battle, some prefer to stay on the sidelines of a fight permanently. Some are not sure which side to choose. Maybe it doesn't seem clear that joining a side will end in much good to anyone. It does seem clear that God alone is our Provider and our ultimate Protector. Is there a need to prepare for battle?

As the business saying goes, "Failing to prepare means you're preparing to fail." It was a grim medieval reality that farmers often bore the brunt of constant warfare between knights battling over the crops in their fields and then demanding follow-up care. Lords of manors clashed over many reasons. Fields would get overrun with soldiers and thieves, or carefully preserved winter stores would be raided. Lone sheep are no match for a coordinated effort of invaders, but a well-organized group with early-warning systems can offer deterrent value.

Since good and evil are in continual warfare, with short periods of peace, it does not seem likely that avoiding war can be a lifelong strategy. Even if you have been living as a Kenite and at peace with the king of Canaan, you may be called to take a side at some point (Judges 4). Most likely this won't involve hammering a tent peg into anyone's temples, but it's certain that niceness is a worse-than-useless defense against a determined and ruthless enemy.

So instead, you must prepare:

1. **Communicate with your leaders and community.** Church organizations often have varying levels of higher authorities or appeal, so use the chain of command, whether it's a court system or a board of trustees. Alongside Matthew 18 rules, the information must follow the proper channels. This protects your

own integrity as well as the health and welfare of the organization. Your conscience must be clear.

2. **Trust and patience.** Unless the situation absolutely requires speed, be prepared to speak, and then leave the outcome in God's hands. This does not mean that the only option is to sit on your hands, pray, and just let the Lord sort it out. It does mean that continual agitation can ruin potential progress.

3. **Exceptions.** Consider using an exception as a last resort, because exceptions are often used by malcontents to get their way.[25] Wolves do get revealed over time, sometimes by prayer and fasting, and sometimes when the flock gets a Jonathan who is willing to climb up hillsides and take on the Philistines (1 Samuel 14).

4. **Last option.** Do all in your power to respectfully warn the powers that be (Romans 13, Hebrews 13, and I Peter 2). As per Ezekiel 33, if those you have warned do not heed the warning, on their own heads be it. Your job has been done, if you've followed scriptural mandates lived out by Christ and the Apostle Paul in their court cases. The real advantage of sounding an alarm is that you can't be reproached later on. If you follow the process through to the end, even if it causes personal hurt, you can say that you exhausted all of the available means of addressing a real issue.

---

[25] The Scottish Reformation story of Jenny Geddes (throwing her folding stool at the head of a minister) illustrates the frustration of congregants forced to listen to the Common Book of Prayer in worship services; I heard a wolf try to use this historical resistance point to justify his anti-authoritarian behavior.

Let's say the wolves have taken over all leadership positions, they won't be expelled by the flock, and there are no appeals left. If the synagogue has been turned over to Satan, it's time to leave. Do not take this step lightly, nor without real prayer and a double-check of your motives from at least one disinterested third party. Sometimes the best option is to leave after all other options have been exhausted. Far too many church refugees and malcontents can drag every acquaintance into a tell-all about their terrible experiences with the church. God called us to be pilgrims in tents, but He didn't call us to live outside of a community of believers.

5. **Refuse to be eaten alive by guilt or doubt.** Satan and his children are master manipulators. They know how to transfer responsibility so their issue becomes all. your. fault. While allowing room for the Spirit's work in discerning your own sin, neglect, or stubbornness, do not allow illegitimate authorities a position of power over you. Do not concede to them the right to tell you how you should be if they, themselves, refuse any checks and balances from authorities over them.

6. **Withstand authorities respectfully.** While Paul was speaking as an officer of an ecclesiastical court in saying, *"We did not yield submission to them for even an hour"* (Galatians 2:5), it's possible to have this attitude while remaining true to your own authority structure. Remember that being treated badly is no excuse for bad behavior. If every single one of your earthly authorities has become caught up in the general madness, a la Peter suddenly avoiding Gentiles when Jewish delegates came to town, it may be necessary to call them out on their hypocrisy. Respect to authorities

cannot be overemphasized in this anti-authoritarian age, especially when sin makes it so easy to become individual *"judges with evil thoughts"* (James 2:4) about how everyone is wrong except for (the idolatrous) me. If you can show submission to God and to no one's guilt trip, that's a good indicator that you're on the right track.

Having Done All, Stand Firm in Your Faith

If you have defeated a wolf—celebrate. It's an accomplishment. Defeating a wolf can be a real victory that discourages or limits further damage, but it is not the end. The ultimate victory is with Christ, who has already defeated Death. He has provided the Spirit who helps us overcome sin. It will ultimately be defeated by a combination of the cross and the Last Judgment. A victory on Earth is a reflection of God's triumph over His enemies.

However, when it looks like the battle has been lost, don't despair—it's one battle. The war is not over, and He has declared us to be more than conquerors. For the sake of your own sanity and faith, if you have gone to the very edge of proclaiming the truth that no one wants to hear—it's okay to just stand firm, having done everything you can.

God's Word states that destroyers will get the ultimate punishment. As with Daniel's false accusers, eventually the wolves will reap exactly what they have sown (Daniel 6:24). They spread false accusations, they wanted Daniel to be torn apart—they became food for lions.

APPENDIX:
SECULAR CASE STUDIES

Secular Case Study #1: Fyre Festival 2017

Leaders: Billy McFarland + Ja Rule
Based on *FYRE: The Greatest Party That Never Happened*

While the main focus of this work remains on wolves within the flock of believers, it's sometimes instructive to describe a very current scenario within the business world that has implications for the church world. Consider this a modern-day parable.

The marketing disaster surrounding the 2017 Fyre Festival is a good example of a charismatic leader, a generation who craves identity within community, and the desire to believe that castles in the air can be formed into reality. As churches get ever more enamored of the world's methods of "success," this sort of mentality leading to brokenness (of dreams, hearts, and promises) has become increasingly common.

In the business world, people are often encouraged to launch themselves boldly and recklessly into a world of their own creation. It's the old Tower of Babel routine: man's attempt to replace God by becoming the creator of a new and better reality. Any voices encouraging the team to be grounded in reality can be decried as "negative" (i.e., lacking in faith) and dismissed on that basis. "We want solutions, not endless problems" is the cry, mixed with "Now let's see how we can get [these arbitrary goals] done! Progress! Onwards!" Any industry experts who describe the plan as unrealistic can be dismissed as old, tired thinking that has no place in a brave trend-setting world. "We'll show everyone that the impossible can be done."

This is pie-in-the-sky contrarian thinking at its worst. The media and music world already thrive on the creation of money (a tangible asset) out of something ethereal and intangible, tapping into groups' dissatisfaction tied to deep emotion and longing for identity. The Fyre Festival was just an extreme version of smoke-and-mirrors marketing that gets sold in boardrooms across the country.

A rising entrepreneur, Billy McFarland, and a prominent rap artist, Ja Rule, combined forces, convinced they would be the next "Magic Bird" winning combination, based on Larry Bird and Magic Johnson. They decided to turn a cocaine dealer's private Bahamian island into a music festival paradise, a Woodstock 2.0; the Christian equivalent would be to turn a large (former) strip club or drug dealer's den into a church campus.

In the face of endless issues and lack of planning, both leaders kept assuring employees and contractors to just trust the vision (have faith) and keep moving forward with solutions, essentially bringing order out of chaos. Any dose of reality offered by the team members regarding inadequate sewage or housing, unrealistic deadlines, and lack of funds was met with endlessly cheery optimism. Millions were sunk into the project. It was "necessary" for the festival to move forward so the leaders could pay their bills and avoid prison time for selling a false dream.

In cases of stubborn resistance, the positive response would include former successes trotted out as evidence; the Christian version would be misapplied maxims about God's miraculous support for David or Daniel in time of need. A negative response would lead to the voice of resistance being fired; in a church context, this would mean excommunication from the community. The Fyre employees were driven to bouts of despair followed by a heroic output of activity, constantly putting out fires and frantically trying to come up with solutions.

One manager became fully prepared to bribe a government official by the use of his own body, a really twisted rendering of "do not grow weary in doing good" (Galatians 6:9). All of these efforts and round-the-clock attempts to create a partiers' paradise on Earth were not enough.

Every warning sign pointing toward a collapsing dream was ignored. When the island deal fell through, the top leaders resorted to an immense amount of selective reporting. The Fyre Festival creators never told the ticket holders that the entire plan was baseless since they had ignored the advice of industry experts. They pretended that the portion of another island they secured, 45 days before the festival, was both private and exclusive. They reposted old footage of talent shoots taken months earlier from the promotional tour rather than showing any new progress. Any negative reviews and social media comments from ticket holders were deleted in order to keep public concern down to a dull roar. Behind the scenes was daily chaos and the daily question: Should we shut it down?

Employees were either being paid wrong amounts or in mysterious sacks of cash; many contractors were left unpaid. Questions stacked up. Billy McFarland, CFO/CEO of a thirty-person media team of employees, would frequently escape to burn off excess stress by furiously driving around a private vehicle— and then return as though nothing had happened. Rumors flew. The charade continued.

A sudden rainstorm destroyed the temporary shelters, awful parodies of the luxury accommodations advertised. And they didn't have a backup plan for the delicate, finicky musical equipment affected by storms. Still, the leaders tried damage control rather than facing up to the inevitable. When the head of marketing drafted a press release trying to shift blame on "circumstances beyond our control," multiple voices told him, "Stop lying. Those circumstances were fully under our control."

After the crowds were herded onto a hastily branded jet airliner (not the luxury flight as promised) and spent six hours milling around being bribed with drinks at a local restaurant, everyone knew something was wrong. After dark, the party mood turned sour as they spied the soaked or sabotaged bedding. Luggage retrieval was a free-for-all, and looting became the norm. A combination of falsified reporting, mismanaged expectations, a web of deceit, lack of oversight and structure, and magical thinking had turned a small society into savage beasts—biting and devouring each other and snatching any supplies available.

Why did the employees stay?

- The CFO/CEO seemed both charismatic and trustworthy; he lit up the room.

- Many well-known celebrities had put their reputations on the line to contribute, fueled by the dream of living like rock stars.

- Many team members had experienced former successes, which seemed like dreams turned into magical reality.

- Each person had already sunk his (or her) personal reputation into the experience by laboring to make the dream become real. Everyone wanted to see some ROI for all the suffering and sleepless nights they had already experienced. Surely it would all turn out right in the end.

After the festival was officially declared a flop, employees fled the island—fearing the retribution of an angry mob of unpaid workers. The CFO later let all the employees go in the most roundabout way possible: stating that they wouldn't get paid but they wouldn't be fired. The cofounder engaged in doublespeak by rejecting employees' assertions that fraud had not happened—only false advertising. That left employees no avenue for filing for unemployment.

McFarland's self-centeredness deepened after he was bailed out at $300,000. He tried to reignite some of the old marketing fire through a twenty-three-year-old front man, selling a VIP experience for eye-catching shows and experiences that had not yet been made public, whose promoters knew nothing about the faux VIP packages. Instead of trying to create a new experience, McFarland tried to piggyback off others' established successes. He eventually pled guilty to fraud and received a six-year sentence.

This type of scenario not only happens when the world is forced to face unwelcome boundaries; it frequently happens in churches where magical thinking is pervasive. "We can do anything through Christ who strengthens us" and "If you ask a mountain to move, it will move" combined with the unscriptural mantra, "Whatever man can think and believe, he can achieve." This completely ignores the Biblical principle that man is a created being who must live according to the rules set down by God from antiquity. God is not required to answer either to man's hope, panic, or expectations.

Magical thinking in the church tries to put words in God's mouth and manage any negative press by pretending that forgiveness means no real consequences for rejecting His word and His character. It is a deadly avenue for genuine believers to be hurt badly by being sold a false package of hope rooted in this world, or a twisted version of what God will provide in the next. Those who were fooled often become determined to avoid any reminders of the experience—once bitten, twice shy.

Secular Case Study #2: Theranos

Leader: Elizabeth Holmes
Based on *The Inventor: Out for Blood in Silicon Valley* (HBO)
Single-minded vision.
Saving lives and money.

A young, female idealist focused on a mission—to disrupt the established, outdated medical technology.

One medical startup, Theranos, blended these themes that resonate with our culture at a most fundamental level. Add a tie-in to the founder's roots in national history (a daughter of the American Revolution) and her noble purpose of helping others, and watch the idea seeds take root.

The idea was rather simple: create an inexpensive blood testing service, using small finger prick samples, to test for a wide range of conditions. Essentially, 30-year-old CEO Elizabeth Holmes's message was that we, the people, can move toward a world without suffering. If only tests were less burdensome, we could get medical conditions diagnosed sooner and cheat death by never saying goodbye before we were ready. Patients would be able to order tests themselves instead of waiting for doctor approval. Holmes used phrases like "actionable health care" and "basic human right" to cement the appeal of this new, revolutionary technology. She gathered a protective ring of older, wiser investors with vast levels of experience and solid family ties, which gave her a patina of unearned authority.

In ten years' time, the company's worth was rated at around $9 billion; it was seen as a serious competitor against the $75 billion lab giants Quest and Laboratory Corporation of America. Walgreens allowed Theranos centers in 41 of its pharmacies, based on test results.

In 2015, the FDA approved one of the tests. By 2018, it was clear that the company's much-publicized success stories were largely fake.

If the background research is correct, there was no investigation into company financial statements because Holmes's word was taken on trust, largely due to her grandfather's network and financial pull. For any new company, issues with product quality concerns plus underlying financial trouble spell disaster.

The HBO commentators were quick to intone that science, facts, and data haven't failed—in this instance, the mostly male investors bought a lie based on an emotional appeal. They, too, can succumb to charm.

- Former political leaders (George Schultz and Henry Kissinger, former Secretaries of State)

- Former Senators, William Frist and Sam Nunn

- Wells Fargo CEO, Dick Bossovitch

- Various retired military leaders (General James Mattis, Gary Roughead)

- The Walmart family (Waltons)

- Media giant Rupert Murdoch

- Tim Draper, family friend and investor (Hotmail, Tesla, Skype, and Baidu)

There was also the pull of desire to be led by a millennial genius, a once-in-a-century "member of a monastic order," as she was described by Henry Kissinger. The problem with this millennial genius was that Ms. Holmes didn't listen to anyone else's advice. At age 18, when a clinical pharmacologist at Stanford told Elizabeth Holmes that her skin patch idea was a nonstarter, she responded with an incredulous look-through-you stare. Obviously, Holmes's next move was to drop out of her studies in chemical engineering and start her own company because the experts sold out to the system were just too hidebound to recognize when someone was working smarter rather than harder.

Holmes was able to craft a policy of tight control around Theranos. The company culture was based on secrecy, "free from outside interference" and therefore free of oversight or third-party verification. The rationale offered by the media was that the venture failed due to lack of specialization and education—if her technicians had been trained in sound medical practice, failure could have been avoided.

Holmes took a gamble based on the idea of man living for eternity, overcoming natural limitations by willpower. Her hero, the inventor Thomas Edison, spent a large part of his life as a fraud who used the media to fuel his dream. He spent four years claiming he'd solved the electric bulb filament issue without ever providing proof. While he was able to avoid bankruptcy by a very narrow margin, she wasn't able to hide the ineffectiveness of her testing device (The Edison).

Visionaries often have a megalomaniac approach, playing God with literal life and death. They can feed into the desire of the public to avoid a complicated, imbalanced system. When people are treated as guinea pigs, it makes them ripe targets for snake-oil salesmen.

In the church world, the equivalent might be a fresh-face-on-old-orthodoxy approach. This hip new pastor (male or female) has gathered a team of influencers and is beating back the tidal wave of worldliness (materialism) with a persuasive blend of social media, quality musical accompaniment, and positive media coverage—maybe trendy social issues thrown in for current appeal (the environment). For the conservatives, they affirm the legitimacy of the old-path principles, throw in quotes from recognized authors like Charles Spurgeon or R.C. Sproul, and talk about the 10 Commandments. For the liberals, they might point out the flaws in conservative methodology, throw in quotes from Timothy Keller, Noam Chomsky, and Martin Luther King, and talk about the need for love and understanding. Everyone can take what they like from the offering presented. Some will grumble that sides aren't being taken, while others rejoice that in Jesus, no sides are needed.

Taking assertions at face value denies the requirement of results and assumes that advertising is truthful. If "wisdom is justified by her children," then earthly products and services should be able to show a level of effectiveness in the light of day. Bending reality only works in a land of fantasy or in completely controlled environments—and because of the human factor, there is always a breach in security somewhere.

Reference List

Available upon request (visit www.coramconversations.com)

www.ingramcontent.com/pod-product-compliance
Lightning Source LLC
Chambersburg PA
CBHW061749120626
46550CB00005B/1943